The Road to Champagne

The Road to Champagne

13 Principles to Drive Career Success

Alejandro Colindres Frañó

BUSINESS EXPERT PRESS

Leader in applied, concise business books

First published in 2022 by
Business Expert Press, LLC
222 East 46th Street, New York, NY 10017
www.businessexpertpress.com

ISBN-13: 978-1-63742-236-6 (paperback)
ISBN-13: 978-1-63742-237-3 (e-book)

Business Expert Press Business Career Development Collection

First edition: 2022

10 9 8 7 6 5 4 3 2 1

To my mom, Isabel, and dad, Marco Antonio, for teaching me many valuable lessons that made my journey possible, and to my wife, Erika, for being an integral part of that journey.

Description

The goal of *The Road to Champagne: 13 Principles to Drive Career Success* is to empower millions of professionals throughout the world to accelerate career growth! Too many smart and well-educated young professionals struggle simply because they lack powerful insights on how to address the main root causes of slow growth. This book presents actionable principles to remove those root causes.

The principles come alive into a well-structured framework illustrated with real stories from the trajectory of successful colleagues and the author's experiences. This pragmatic career guide for young professionals is a product of rigorous problem-solving but is written in a style that is easy to follow.

This book is perfect for any professional with room to grow; hence, it will help those starting their career (including students, recent grads, and those who are a few years into their career), as well as more seasoned professionals with untapped growth potential.

As you know, Champagne represents a celebration of success, achievement, and joy. Success is about arriving at a stage where one's passion, strengths, and interests intersect ... a stage worth celebrating. It also refers to the author's journey in the food and beverage industry across the continent; after working in multiple sectors, he currently enjoys working at a $20B+ distributor of fine Champagne, wine, and spirits in the United States as Vice President of Strategy and Commercial Effectiveness.

Keywords

career; growth; mindset; leadership; professional; success; principles; self-help; Champagne

Contents

Testimonials

"*Getting from where you are, to where you want to be in your career can feel confusing and overwhelming. Alejandro has written the ultimate tool guide to understanding how you can achieve your next steps, with actionable and powerful advice to navigate you through the process! My advice is to read this book and follow through to reach your highest potential possible!*"
—**Dr. Marshall Goldsmith, New York Times #1 bestselling author of** *Triggers, Mojo,* **and** *What Got You Here Won't Get You There,* **Thinkers 50 #1 Executive Coach**

"*Is your career growing at the pace you expected? Are you in the quest for a framework to ensure that you have career mobility throughout your professional life? Alejandro offers a practical guide for intentionality—in setting aspirations, knowing yourself, making connections and mobilizing your professional brand. This guide, enhanced by Alejandro's personal story, offers real-life examples of 13 principles of career success.*"
—**Liza Kirkpatrick, Assistant Dean at Kellogg School of Management's Career Management Center**

"*Reading this career book should be a rite of passage for every young professional. As a recent college graduate, it empowered me to take on the professional world with a much higher level of preparation and is allowing me to maintain a growth mindset as I advance in my career.*"—**Sasha Matera-Vatnick, Associate at Cargill**

"*This is so good! Thorough. Thought-provoking. Transformative. While meant for early career professionals, Champagne is apropos for any stage— and great fodder if you're mentoring others. Through honest, timely anecdotes, shrewd data, and hands-on calls to action, this writer equips you with right-now tools. You'll never look at your career the same way. Buckle up and get ready to own your journey.*"—**Cliff Goins III, Principal of Business Development at Amazon**

"The Road to Champagne *helps you understand—in a unique way—how to build the skills and adopt the behaviors to get you to a different level.*"
—**Guilherme Weege, CEO at Grupo Malwee**

"*I like the simplicity and practicality of the ideas and principles that Alejandro shares. Following these will not only benefit your career, but also your personal growth … no matter what stage you are in.*"—**Chris Callieri, Chief Supply Chain Officer at Tory Burch**

"*This gem is perfect for me in my career right now and will help me better position myself for growth and success.*"—**Angelica Alvarez, HR Program Manager at SGWS**

"The Road to Champagne's *framework is unique in that it helps young professionals not only to advance in their careers, but to do so in a way that brings their passions together for sustainable and balanced growth.*"
—**Megan Prichard, Vice President of Ridesharing Business Unit at General Motors**

"*A practical guide to success as a leader and manager. Alejandro uses his international experience to excellent effect with vivid examples and actionable planning sections. The right attitude, self-knowledge, and proactivity are a powerful cocktail for success anywhere in the world.*"
—**Dr. Mabel M. Miguel, Professor of Leadership and Management, UNC Chapel Hill**

Acknowledgments

I would like to give thanks to many people that have enabled progress in my career by giving me the opportunity to work for them in Honduras, the United States, and Brazil, who have mentored me, and who have helped open doors. They have taught me many lessons that shaped me:

Rebecca K.	Jeff W.	Ignacio F.
Victor G.	Per H.	Luis B.
Ricardo G.	Leo V.	Paulo M.
Tobis C.	Tony P.	Rodrigo M.
Roberto C.	Matt L.	Stephen VO.
Gerardo T.	Marcos G.	Ray L.
Quico Q.	Carlos C.	Terry A.
Patrick VdB.	Oswaldo N.	Gerry R.
Sean M.	Ilde S.	Lawrence K.

I thank my parents, family, coworkers, friends, and wife for making it a rewarding journey, my professors at the American School of Tegucigalpa, Cornell University, and Kellogg-Northwestern, my friends who let me share a little bit about their own stories, my beta reader volunteers for their insights, my niece Karen Turcios for the internal graphics, and Phil Buckley for guiding me through the book publishing process.

Finally, a big thank you to the Business Expert Press team for believing in my message and allowing me to share it.

Introduction

How can I continue growing in my career?
How can I make the next interesting move happen?

These are questions that often come to my mind. These days, I am better prepared to answer them. However, a few years ago, I wondered how my young professional nieces and nephews found those answers and who was guiding them through the career thought process. Thus, the idea for this book was born when I gave them clear, structured advice on how they should manage and navigate their career to become successful. I realized that such advice should reach a broader audience, because everything I told them applies to you too.

Over the past 30 years, I've had quite a journey since graduating from high school (gulp!), and my professional and personal experiences from across the continent have shown me a few key things: we all have room for continued growth and advancement—and relevant knowledge can help us accelerate toward the success we strive for.

I want to help make your journey—the journey of growth in your career—more efficient. In this book you'll find a set of game-changing principles that have been instrumental in my career and life: the 13 principles of career success. I swear by these principles because they pave the way for me to achieve and continue achieving my career goals, and I have witnessed the power of these principles in the lives of many others too. None of these principles are Earth-shattering or new. In fact, they have been there waiting for us to tap into them!

If you're a young professional wanting to grow in your profession or field, this book will show you how. The younger you absorb and implement the principles, the better off you will be. It's like saving and investing for retirement: The younger you start, the more comfortable your retirement. But you must eventually start doing it regardless of your age—there is value to be found here if you are more mature, too (directly plus indirectly if you mentor younger professionals).

Whether you're a college student or recent grad, a business school student or recent MBA, a young professional in a small or large organization, an aspiring entrepreneur or even a seasoned executive with room for growth, this book is for you. It doesn't matter whether you are in industry, government, an NGO, or a small business owner aspiring to be the best in your city, these principles work.

These principles are like the laws of physics—they apply to us all. Speaking about the laws of physics, this book will help you actively overcome a force that affects many: Career inertia. This means that varying levels of energy or effort will be required from you for each principle to bear fruit. In doing so, you'll find the place where your passions intersect.

Let me tell you a bit about me. I was born and raised in Tegucigalpa, the capital of Honduras, in Central America. I am the youngest of four. My father was a civil engineer who owned a construction company and built almost a hundred bridges all over the country, and my mother left her accounting career early on to raise us. Although I was born in one of the poorest countries in the hemisphere, I had the privilege and blessing to attend the best school in my country, the American School of Tegucigalpa.

This opened my eyes to the outside world and somewhat prepared me for Cornell University (I'll explain the "somewhat" in Chapter 3) where I studied food science—which explains my path in the food and beverage industry. I received my MBA from the Kellogg School of Management at Northwestern University, majoring in management and strategy, and marketing. I completed multiple executive education courses at Harvard University, Harvard Business School, MIT Sloan School of Management, The Wharton School, and Fundação Getulio Vargas in Brazil.

For about 25 years, I've worked as a management consultant in prestigious firms and in the food and beverage industry across different sectors in family-owned, public, and private equity held companies ranging from $10M to $48B in annual revenues, in multiple countries, as illustrated in Figure I.1.

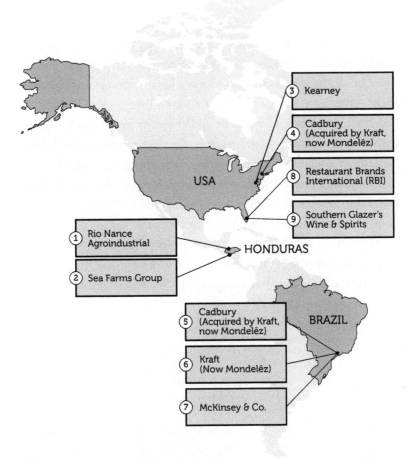

Figure I.1 Alejandro's trajectory

This diverse career trajectory exposed me to many lessons about professional and personal growth, leadership, and career management.

No, I'm not a famous CEO or a wealthy entrepreneur. You can read about Satya Nadella or Elon Musk elsewhere. Why should you listen to *my* advice? Because I am an expert problem solver who analyzed why most professionals are "here" when they have the potential to be "there." And I have achieved exciting goals in my career that have made me successful, and I am not done growing. Oh, and very importantly, I have also made mistakes in managing my career growth, as we all have.

What is success?

How do I define success? Success is not reaching the highest possible step in your hierarchy, because if that was true, only one person in a 10,000-people organization would be successful. In my case, success means being able to proactively construct a life that sets me up for growth where my passions intersect—what I do for a living, what organization I do it for, and where I live ... are all defined by my desires and interests. What's more, this should result in financial prosperity too. What's the point of being passionate about work but not being financially free? Fulfillment and prosperity can and *should* go together. The 13 principles are helping me achieve the intersection of my passions because they allow me to control my career much better than without them.

So, what does it mean to actively construct a life where your passions intersect? It means living the life you want without making major sacrifices, and you are in the sweet spot where the following elements intersect, as shown in Figure I.2.

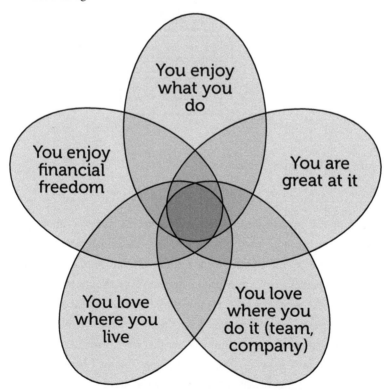

Figure I.2 Alejandro's definition of professional success

It's similar to "Ikigai" but expanded, because to me, living where you want to live is also a huge element. For many years, I enjoyed *some* of these elements, while the others were a conscious sacrifice. Sounds familiar? I lived in cities that I didn't necessarily love, but that's where the right experiences I needed at that time were found. Do you think this tropical teenager wanted to be in Ithaca, New York? Absolutely not. I wanted to live in a beach town and surf after class, but I recognized that Cornell would likely be more effective in shaping my future opportunities, especially in the food industry. So, I ended up buying winter clothes instead of wetsuits and walked 20 minutes to class through -40°F winds on my worst winter morning walk (I learned -40°F equals -40°C the hard way). My dreams of surfing were replaced with snowboarding.

I worked in roles where I felt underpaid, but I knew that a temporary "investment in my growth" would eventually position me for better paid positions. I worked in functions where I didn't see myself staying for long, but I had to excel there to acquire new skills that would be useful down the road. No, I do not enjoy procurement and I would never build a career out of it, but it helped sharpen my negotiation skills and allowed me to work with most countries in Latin America and the Caribbean, which I loved.

The 13 principles have taken me on an exciting journey across top schools and leading companies in multiple countries. They have enabled me to reach an exciting phase: Working in commercial strategy in a multibillion dollar division of an industry-leading company—a division that houses an iconic and prestigious Champagne portfolio!

Why Champagne?

Why Champagne? As you know, Champagne represents a celebration of success, achievement, and joy. It's present when a driver wins the challenging race or when your loved ones get married. A couple of years ago, I drove from Munich to Alsace and then to Champagne via the beautiful and curvy Vosges Mountains to visit Champagne houses while on vacation with my wife. Figuratively speaking, I also drove my career through an exciting and winding road to this Champagne stage I am enjoying. I want you to find your Champagne too, by being better equipped to get there.

Now, I can honestly say that my passions intersect perfectly because I:

- **Work in commercial strategy as a vice president.** I help our business make the best choices across multiple strategic issues. This is what I excel at, and I get high satisfaction from solving complex problems that have a real impact on the business and steering the leadership team toward the optimal solution. I am leveraging the consulting toolkit I created after demanding and mind-shaping years at Kearney, McKinsey, and RBI.
- **Work at the best and largest U.S. distributor of Champagne, wine, and spirits.** Keyword: *Champagne!* Since taking an introductory wine course in college in 1994, I have evolved into a wine aficionado. Visiting wine regions has been an idyllic vacation for over 20 years. The last one was Provence, the next one will be Douro Valley.
- **Live in Miami.** No more ice scraper in my trunk, closer to my family, and a beautiful beach lifestyle. I had my eyes on Miami since 2003 when I lived in Alexandria, VA. It took me over a decade to finally settle here! I was in Brazil before that and limited my U.S. job search to nothing north of Ft. Lauderdale. It worked: now I have palm trees outside my window and the Caribbean as my backyard.

Are you asking yourself why I didn't wait until I progressed further in my career, becoming a senior vice president or C-suite executive before I wrote this book, to impress you with a bigger title? It's simple. I believe that the same principles I can share with you now are the ones I would share with you 2 to 10 years down the road, whenever my career peaks. I'll do it now to benefit you sooner!

The Road to Champagne is not about reaching a final destination. It's about getting to the next phase where you enjoy more success: A phase worth celebrating … so pop some bubbly! What's next for me after this exciting phase? I hope it's related to wines and Champagne, but I don't know; It should be something that expands my success and continues to give me more of what I seek for.

The framework

This framework will help you get to the next stage more efficiently, and to have more momentum to accelerate continued growth. The framework is simple and easy to understand. It might not be easy to execute, though, as it requires effort—how much depends on how proficient you currently are at each principle. But you already know success doesn't come easy. Through the framework of the 13 principles, you'll appreciate how each principle is relevant to you, see real examples of each principle at work, and develop specific actions to start activating each principle in your life.

There are three parts to this book, where we'll explore:

1. What mindset will help propel you forward
2. How you should build and manage your professional brand
3. How you can become your own driver

The following Figure I.3 introduces the framework that ties these parts and 13 principles together.

So, what's your Champagne? Where do you want to arrive? Buckle up and start your engine: We're going to explore the framework that will help you accelerate toward a better phase in your career. Let's do this!

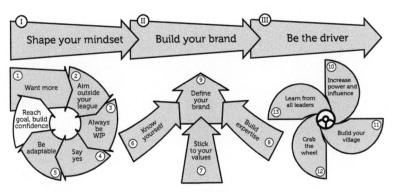

Figure I.3 The Road to Champagne© framework

If you don't go after what you want, you will never have it. If you don't ask, the answer is always no. If you don't step forward, you're always in the same place.

> —Nora Roberts, American romance novel author

Reading suggestions

- Read the chapters in chronological order to walk through the framework in the most logical manner.
- Don't just read through: Pause to reflect when asked a question. There is space for you to jot down your thoughts and responses.
- For maximum benefit, complete the Actions at the end of each chapter. They are intended to help you convert the concepts to concrete steps to make the principle a reality in your life.
- Complete the Self-Assessment exercise at the end of each chapter. This will help you prioritize which principles to focus your improvement efforts on, as explained in the Self-Assessment section at the end of the book.

PART I

Shape Your Mindset

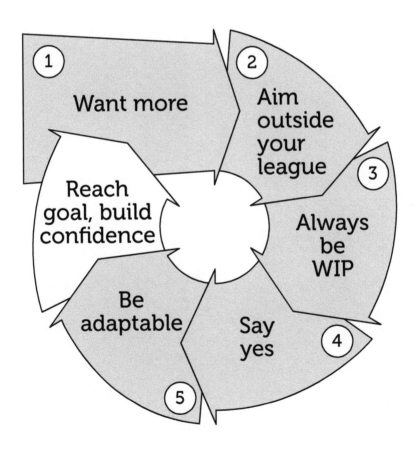

CHAPTER 1

Want More

When you achieve one dream, dream another. Getting what you want is only a problem if you have nowhere to go next. Dreaming is a lifetime occupation.

—Rudy Ruettiger, American motivational speaker and author

Why Should You?

"How can I continue growing in my career? How can I make the next interesting move happen?" The underlying premise of these questions is that I can do something about where my career is headed. If I had no control over my career, I would not waste my time pondering this. But I do, and you do too! And it all starts with our mindset, which may require reprogramming—fortunately though, our mindset can change, evolve, and improve. The biggest and most important premise I have about why you should read this book is that "more" is possible and achievable in your career and life.

More what? More knowledge, responsibility, impact, diverse experiences, fulfillment, autonomy, control over your life, international exposure, prosperity, or happiness, for example. "More" should not be a greedy proposition focused on accumulating money: That will come when you achieve more of some of the elements I listed. When you make money your sole mission, you risk making costly and poor decisions.

You must determine what it is that you want more of. Only then can you try to find out *where* you can get it, and then *how* to get there. What you want more of will evolve as you mature. For example, early in my career, I wanted more responsibility and opportunities to gain experience, then I also wanted emerging market experience, later I wanted more work-life balance, and so on. That's normal. But figure out what you want more of now.

To grow in our career, we need the right mindset, and wanting more is the first step in shaping our mindset. It is an acknowledgment that we still have many yards to go to reach the goal line. However, many people do not actively want more. Many indeed wish for more, but they place no effort behind the desire. As you will see, all principles we'll cover require action (at least I haven't been able to just think my way to success), and it starts with this one. The principles are simple, but not exactly easy to execute—wanting more requires the right balance: Too little doesn't bring growth, too much can lead to frustrations and lack of peace of mind.

So, why do many not want more in their career or life? There are several potential answers, but here are three key reasons:

- They do not believe more is possible. Their frame of reference does not allow them to see all the real possibilities out there: Their current mindset limits their vision. They think their current stage is the goal line because they lack guidance from others that can help them see what's out there waiting for them.
- They are too focused on the present. The present stage can be comfortable—they know it well and it's not bad. That comfort zone prevents them from dreaming about what's next.
- They consider change risky. Anything that comes next implies change, and change is not welcome by many, as we will explore in Chapter 5.

The danger is that by not wanting more, people fall into a trap of stagnation: Career inertia. When they don't want more, their journey is pretty much done, and they prematurely reach their end goal. If young, this is not a good way to live—too much wasted potential! They go on living their lives foregoing all the big possibilities ... if they only opened their eyes and minds to them. And that, my friends, is a scary thought. On the flip side, when you are obsessively consumed by wanting more, you do not enjoy the present and risk being flooded by negative emotions that can derail you. More on that later in this chapter.

When you want more in a balanced and healthy way, you reap certain benefits including:

- It provides the spark that starts a goal-setting process for your career.
- It fuels you to create a plan to work toward the new aspiration.
- Executing against that plan maximizes the probability of you reaching the goal of more.

Therefore, when you want more, strategically plan how to unlock it, and work on your plan, you are opening the door for more to arrive! Wanting more is simply about wanting to unleash your potential and improve your situation.

Why have I wanted more (perhaps a highly visible project or a better job)? Because I believed I was capable of bigger and better achievements—my full potential was untapped. Why did I believe I was capable of more? Well, because I trusted my abilities would allow me to accomplish bigger missions, perhaps proven by recent accomplishments. Self-efficacy, or the trust you have in your potential to perform, leads you to achieve your expected outcome. The contrary is also true, though—fail to believe in yourself and you won't conquer much. What we believe can anchor or propel us! And we don't like anchors when we are trying to accelerate growth, do we?

To want more, some readers need to reshape their mindset, which is possible according to many, including Carol Dweck, a psychology professor at Stanford University. In her book *Mindset*, she explains that the view you adopt for yourself profoundly affects the way you lead your life.[1] She goes on to define a mindset as just a set of beliefs—which can change—and presents two types: The fixed and the growth mindset. Predominantly fixed mindset people try to prove they are talented and to master what they know. Predominantly growth mindset people try to stretch and extend what they know and learn more. As you know, the

---

[1] C.S. Dweck. 2016. *Mindset: The New Psychology of Success.* Ballantine Books.

initial stages of learning make you feel like an amateur. This prevents fixed mindset people from extracting joy out of learning and thus avoiding such experiences.

The author of *There Is More*[2] captures it perfectly when he states, "There is always more ahead of you than you've allowed yourself to dream or allowed yourself to believe."

I do have to point out a major implication of wanting more. Because if I don't, you risk falling into an unpleasant trap that captures many people. Wanting more does not mean you are constantly and permanently dissatisfied with your present state. That awful condition can torture many, and I am not advocating that ... as a matter of fact I want to warn you about it.

Want More, But Be Thankful

Let me start off by publicly acknowledging I have a blessed life. I always try to be grateful and enjoy every stage of my life and career ... all the ups and downs, the victories and failures, moments of pain and joy, career boredom and career excitement, everything. Of course, I've faced many struggles and disappointments just like everyone else ... but that doesn't change how I feel about my life. And I would propose you are pretty well-blessed and privileged too. I mean, here you are, exploring how to accelerate growth in your career, when many people we know (and billions we don't know) don't have the health, education, drive, or means to focus on exciting career possibilities. In our lives there are dozens of privileges others wish they had, not just things we lack. Where we focus our minds on—what we have or what we lack—is a critical decision with significant consequences.

A study by "The Journal of Personality and Social Psychology"[3] concluded "Results suggest that a conscious focus on blessings may have emotional and interpersonal benefits." It lists these benefits of gratitude:

---

[2] B. Houston. 2018. *There Is More*. WaterBrook.

[3] R.A. Emmons and M.E. McCullough. 2003. "Counting Blessings Versus Burdens: An Experimental Investigation of Gratitude and Subjective Well-Being in Daily Life." *The Journal of Personality and Social Psychology* 84, no.2, pp. 377–389.

- Increases well-being as it builds psychological, social, and spiritual resources.
- Inspires prosocial reciprocity and altruism.
- Builds and strengthens social bonds and friendships.
- Broadens the scope of cognition and enables flexible and creative thinking.
- Facilitates coping with stress and adversity.
- Increases the likelihood that people will function optimally and feel good in the future.

Other sources list even more benefits, including better sleep ("Gratitude predicted greater subjective sleep quality and sleep duration, and less sleep latency and daytime dysfunction"),4 better health ("Patients expressing more gratitude also had lower levels of inflammatory biomarkers"),5 and even love life ("Gratitude had uniquely predictive power in relationship promotion, perhaps acting as a booster shot for the relationship").6 On the flip side, I have seen quite negative effects in people who focus on what they lack, including deteriorated health and imploded peace of mind. Perhaps you've also noticed that?

So, wanting more does not contradict being grateful, they can coexist. Understanding this balance will better equip you for your journey. Based on decades of observing those around me, I propose there are four types of people, based on two variables as depicted in Figure 1.1.

We all fall into one of the four zones in the matrix, at any given moment. You can identify which of the four groups others fall into based on their happiness level, what they talk about, and even their outlook on life. Let's explore each of the four zones in the matrix (notice each is numbered), and let's do it counter clockwise:

---

4 A.M. Wood et al. January 2009. "Gratitude Influences Sleep Through the Mechanism of Pre-sleep Cognitions." *Journal of Psychosomatic Research* 66, no. 1.
5 P.J. Mills et al. 2015. "The Role of Gratitude in Spiritual Well-being in Asymptomatic Heart Failure Patients." *Spirituality in Clinical Practice* Vol. 2, No. 1, pp. 5–17. American Psychological Association.
6 S.B. Algoe et al. 2010. "It's the Little Things: Everyday Gratitude as a Booster Shot for Romantic Relationships." *Personal Relationships* 17, pp. 217–233.

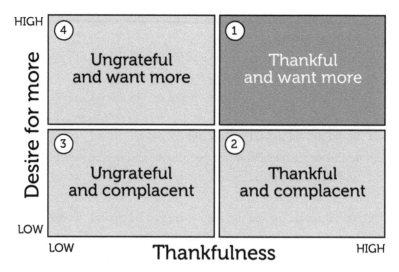

Figure 1.1 Want More Matrix

The downside of believing you will be happy when you achieve your next goal—and get more—is that you could spend all or most of your life feeling unfulfilled and unhappy ... because hopefully there will always be a next goal to aim for. Author Dr. Marshall Goldsmith, in his bestseller *What Got You Here Won't Get You There*, refers to the tendency of believing happiness is conditional upon certain achievements (i.e., getting that promotion, making more money, and so on) as the Great Western Disease. Yes, we need to be better at detaching our level of happiness from our bank account statement, net worth calculation, or accomplishment checklist. Let's enjoy and appreciate the present, even if imperfect.

Zone #4: Ungrateful and Want More. People here want to do something to continue evolving and improving: Awesome! However, they are *typically* more worried, stressed, and overwhelmingly dissatisfied compared to people in Zone #1 and #2—on the right side of the matrix. Many of them have a lot of positive things going on in their lives. But they overlook them and just focus on what they don't have, causing a lot of unnecessary pain and stress. They believe they will be happy when they get that more.

Zone #3: Ungrateful and Complacent. Worst zone to be in, because they are sitting idle and comfortably, yet focused on what they don't have. They complain a lot but fail to do something about whatever is unsatisfactory in their career or life. They are equally exposed to the negative emotions affecting those in Zone #4.

Zone #2: Thankful and Complacent. People here appreciate what's working well for them but miss out on many great opportunities simply because they have settled into their current comfortable circumstances. Of course, there is a healthy *temporary* presence in Zone #2: For example, when you just achieved a goal and will savor it before planning the next one. When I move into a new role, my sole focus is to prove myself by learning and delivering results, not yet worrying about the next move. At some point though, after mastering that role (which takes over a year), I want more. But many people get too comfortable and grow roots in Zone #2.

Zone #1: Thankful and Want More. In my life—and in the lives of people I admire—what has worked is having that attitude of appreciation and enjoyment of the present stage but matched with a desire to take a step further and build upon those blessings and achievements to take my life into an even better future stage. I realize we may have different religious or spiritual beliefs, that's perfectly fine, but allow me to shed light on *my* thought process so you understand better my perspective. As a Christian, I thank God for whatever happens to me that day and week ... and then I pray for wisdom and endurance to achieve further growth and advancement. Philippians 4:6 says, "Do not be anxious about anything, but in every situation, by prayer and petition, with thanksgiving, present your requests to God." Because the word *thanksgiving* is only separated by a comma from *present your requests,* I do not see a conflict between enjoying the present circumstances and wanting more.

But you don't need to share my spiritual beliefs to appreciate the power of thankfulness, the scientific research outlined earlier explained it clearly! Zone #1 is the healthiest group to fall into: You benefit from the peace-of-mind of appreciating what you have, plus you continuously improve your world.

So, after reflecting on the matrix ... which quadrant best describes you now? The good news is we can control what group we are in. If you are not in Zone #1, you can move your way into it by adopting small yet impactful changes.

Move toward the right in the matrix by being more thankful:

- Every day pause and appreciate your current situation. Despite multiple difficulties and things you wish you had, you have a lot of things working in your favor. Express gratitude for what you have.
- Many suggest documenting such a list in a daily journal for a few weeks. Give it a try. I am not the journal type, so I do it in my daily prayers. Just do it somehow.
- Watch what comes out of your mouth. Words of gratitude or complaints? Bite your tongue when complaining and learn to focus on the gratitude list.
- Externalize this by thanking others frequently, even for small things.

Move upwards in the matrix by not growing roots in your present stage and wanting more:

- Identify what aspects of your career and life can improve: What do you want more of? Something you lack? Something in your gratitude list you want to expand?
- Envision being in that state of more. Believe more is possible because it is.

Now that you want more, translate that future-state vision into concrete actions to take.

Refer to the Actions at the end of this chapter for more specific steps—they are meant to encourage you to pause and think about how to apply each principle to your career and life. You can also download free Actions templates in fillable pdf format from www.roadtochampagne.com in The 13 Principles page.

*Reflect on your present blessings, on which every man has many, not
on your past misfortunes, of which all men have some.*
                    —Charles Dickens, British novelist (1812–1870)

Time to Bust Out

After graduating from Cornell University, I happily returned to Honduras
because staying and working in the United States didn't seem tempting at
the time. I missed my friends, family, and my girlfriend Erika who is now
my wife. Plus, I needed a break from the brutal Ithaca winters.

My first job was at a small family-owned fruit processing company as
Quality Control Manager, where I managed a department on day one—a
responsibility not many green college grads get! However, it took me a few
months to figure out internal growth opportunities were absent. I quit
after 11 months and joined one of the most recognized local companies,
Sea Farms Group, a leader in aquaculture in Latin America at that time.
I had a good position as Quality Assurance Manager, performed well, and
formed good relationships with people at all levels within the company.
I was thankful for that and was truly enjoying that stage.

But in Central America, most companies are privately held: Some
countries have a specific number of families (that you can count with
your two hands) that control the economy. After several years, it dawned
on me that despite my solid track record, without the right last name, my
growth was limited—executive positions are generally reserved for family
members or inner circle individuals. I would have to marry somebody's
niece to get the most attractive opportunities. Or change my context to
a more meritocratic one, where rising based on my abilities and having
plenty of exciting opportunities is the norm. I wanted my career to grow
more, but my potential and drive were hitting limiting factors already.

When I was accepted to an MBA program in the United States,
I decided this time I would seek growth opportunities in the United
States. In such business context, my family ties become less relevant and
what matters is what value I create for an organization. Seemed fair to
me! After four years working in my country, I left with no intention of
returning to work. Had I not wanted to grow professionally beyond the

glass ceiling around me, I would still be under it (likely ripping my hair out). But I wanted more, and that unlocked a series of events, twists, turns, achievements, that have made my life richer. It all started with this principle … Want More.

Wrap-Up

The first step in a journey to improve and transform your career or life is to want more; thus, it is a prerequisite to unleash the powers of the other 12 principles. This first step starts in your mind. According to *The Champion's Mind* by Jim Afremow, what separates the top few from the many in a sport is mentality.[7] If this is true for athletes competing on physical strength, ability, and endurance, imagine how much more applicable this is for our nonsports careers where we compete on our mental abilities. He goes on to explain how adopting a winning mindset will help athletes perform at the top of their game and enable them to succeed when they want to succeed the most. A growth mindset and thankful attitude will take you closer to the top of your game—find a home in Zone #1 with just temporary visits to Zone #2. Avoid Zones #3 and #4.

> *Good is the enemy of great. Few people attain great lives, in large part because it is just so easy to settle for a good life.*
>
> —Jim Collins, American business author and speaker

---

[7] J. Afremow. 2013. *The Champion's Mind*. Rodale.

Take-Aways: Want More

- Wanting more is a key assumption when asking *"How can I continue growing in my career? How can I make the next interesting move happen?"*
- Don't settle in or get too comfy, aspire to more in your life.
- You need to know what you want more of.
- What you believe you can achieve helps shape what you achieve.
- Be grateful for what you have and for your current circumstances (you are likely better off than many people around you).

Self-Assessment

Which statement describes you best? Circle the corresponding letter.

a. I struggle with wanting more. My current situation is not bad, so I rarely push myself to seek better opportunities.

b. I generally want more but don't actively seek new ways to grow in my career. As I look back, there are only a few examples of it in my career and life.

c. I have a solid track record of wanting more. I always know I can do bigger things, so I seek growth opportunities: Even now.

Actions

- Think about which group you fall into: I currently fall into Zone #_____.
- Is change needed? In which direction (right, up, or both)?

  _____

- List ten or more aspects of your career and life that you are thankful for:

  o _____

  o _____

  o _____

  o _____

- o _____
- o _____
- o _____
- o _____
- o _____
- o _____
- o _____
- o _____

- List three or more aspects of your life and career that would benefit from improving (you can include aspects from the first list). What do you want more of?

  1. _____
  2. _____
  3. _____
  4. _____

  5. _____

- For each listed above, lay out concrete actions you will take to make that *more* a reality. Add completion dates (create new events in your calendar to be reminded).

  1.   Target date
     - _____ _____
     - _____ _____
     - _____ _____

  2.
     - _____ _____
     - _____ _____
     - _____ _____

  3.
     - _____ _____
     - _____ _____
     - _____ _____

4.

  - _____   _____
  - _____   _____
  - _____   _____

5.

  - _____   _____
  - _____   _____
  - _____   _____

- Envision that future stage of an improved you … realize it is achievable!

CHAPTER 2

Aim Outside Your League

All who have accomplished great things have had a great aim, have fixed their gaze on a goal which was high, one which sometimes seemed impossible.

—Orison Swett Marden, American businessman and author
(1850–1924)

Why Should You?

Setting your aim is a fundamental and critical step in the entire process, and it only comes after deciding you want more. It helps you answer: "How much more?" Much has been proclaimed about the power of dreaming big, and I must emphasize it. There is an extremely direct relationship between how high your aspirations are and how spectacular your achievements are. When your goal is stretched and ambitious, you will be motivated and engaged by the possibility of that future state, you will be driven to find creative ways of achieving it, you will grow more professionally and/or personally, and you will tap into all of your potential. When your goal is average, no additional energy beyond the normal momentum is needed to achieve it: It leads to an easy and inglorious achievement.

When you achieve the high goal, not only did you attain more for your life, you just boosted your self-confidence by recalibrating your mindset on what is possible, and thereby started the virtuous cycle where your newly strengthened self-confidence sets you up for more ambitious goals in your life (remember self-efficacy and the growth mindset from Chapter 1).

Of course, you will not always reach that high goal in your first attempt. If you fail to achieve your high goal, you likely landed in an advantaged spot anyway or learned valuable lessons to consider in the next attempt: Either way, you are still better off than aiming for the comfortable and the expected.

I was the project manager for a margin enhancement project, and Bill, the executive sponsor, remarked; "Let's increase the gross margin of the North American candy category from 34 percent to 60 percent to get closer to the other product categories, in order to justify future investment dollars." For nonfinance readers, that is revenues minus costs divided by revenues, a measure of profitability for that product line. I thought he was joking because that is a hairy and aggressive improvement goal … almost doubling profitability. Perhaps 45 percent is more reasonable, I thought.

After a detailed 100-day diagnostic and months of implementing significant changes to the manufacturing lines, product portfolio, packaging materials, trade spend allocation, and others, we achieved 60 percent! It felt empowering to achieve an ambitious goal, and it reinforced that the only way to achieve spectacular results is by aiming high. If we aimed for 45 percent, we would've likely achieved 45 percent, or perhaps not because it wouldn't have been the type of project to get all functions charged up to be as creative as possible—but we surely wouldn't have reached 60 percent.

There is nothing ground-breaking about this concept. It is basic, but many of us fall in the trap of not aiming high. Why do we limit ourselves? Perhaps because:

- We want to avoid the sour taste of failure.
- We listen to loud voices around us that remind us what is normal for our context—those voices are typically fueled by their own deep complacency, ignorance of the true possibilities out there, and even jealousy of you achieving more than them.
- We don't exactly know what to aspire to, in the absence of guidance.
- We don't feel we have what it takes to achieve the high goal. It will, after all, require a lot of energy, effort, dedication, and sacrifices to achieve an ambitious goal.

I would also add a little bit of luck to that last point, but we'll keep luck out of it since it's out of our control and we'll only focus on what we can control. Let me share a few examples of this principle in my life and Alex's.

Going to Cornell

My first experience with setting ambitious goals was back in high school ... thinking about where to go for college. I decided to go outside my home country for two main reasons: I was not impressed with the academic rigor and quality of the local options and I had the example of my three siblings who studied in the United States—I visited Marco and Ileana when they were students at the University of Texas at Austin, and I visited Luis while he was a student at Louisiana State University in Baton Rouge. Their experiences unconsciously changed my perception of what normal meant: Study abroad.

As the next step, I identified alternatives of where I should apply. I was interested in food science (a fascinating mix of chemistry, microbiology, engineering, and many other fields), because I loved science and the food industry wasn't going away anytime soon. My oldest brother Marco helped me through that thought process. I then researched the best universities offering that major in the United States. I applied to the best three, and to a few other schools lower in the rankings (some safety schools ... you know the strategy). One of the three was Cornell University.

Now, you should understand I was not the most brilliant in my class. I was a B+/A– student, with not-so-stellar extracurricular activities. But I did have some yet-unrefined level of dedication, ambition, discipline, and drive. It must have come across in my multiple essays that complimented my good-but-not-spectacular SAT scores and not-high-enough-but-let-me-try GPA. My SAT score was lower than what usnews.com states is the mid-range: "Half the applicants admitted to Cornell University have an SAT score between 1390 and 1540." The numbers should've intimidated me and stopped me right there, because I didn't hit the acceptance expectations, theoretically. But I am glad I didn't allow that. To this day, I prefer to have somebody else tell me "no." Who am I to say no to myself? An Ivy League admissions member? Of course not, I'll let them do their job. By the way, at this point in my life, a no is likely just the start of a negotiation conversation.

Eventually, I received the fat envelope via mail! I was thrilled to be accepted. I was 17 years old when all this happened, and that was the first time I achieved what others would consider a highly unexpected outcome. But this lesson has stuck with me because it is powerful. Doors will not open if you don't knock on them. My point is this: If you are going to invest time and energy knocking, choose a door that you don't have a high probability of opening: A door that will help transform your life and elevate your career to a new league if it does.

Going to Kellogg

My second experience with this principle happened years later after graduating from Cornell and returning to Honduras. However, someone helped me raise my aim. When I worked as Quality Assurance Manager at FG Mariscos, part of Sea Farms Group, I clearly asked myself "How can I continue growing in my career? How can I make the next interesting move happen?"

Stakeholders selected me to help design and bring to life a new plant (FG Mariscos) that would allow Sea Farms Group to enter the ready-to-eat shrimp market in Europe. It was an energizing phase where I sharpened my technical, team management, and project management skills. With my counterpart Jose, we visited and benchmarked seafood cooking plants in Europe, helped select equipment, helped design the layout and flow, wrote operating manuals, trained the new personnel, and helped bring the new operation to life.

Soon after we completed the mission, I realized that I wanted to get closer to the executive decision-making process. I only helped execute somebody's vision: I did not participate in the strategic conversations that concluded a new plant was required. At that moment, I realized I needed to acquire business skills if I ever wanted to get into the business side of the food industry. That made me think about business school.

I made up my mind, and I applied to INCAE Business School in Costa Rica. I visited my brother Marco when he was getting his MBA there, and liked the campus. It has always been a reputable business school—at times, the best in Latin America according to Financial Times. Harvard professors helped found it in the 1960s.

I was accepted! I spoke to the company's CFO requesting financial assistance for me to attend. Gerardo told me what I am telling you now, by saying: "I discussed this with the executive team, and we would like to support you. But we encourage you to apply to top business schools in the United States."

Why didn't I think of that by myself? I already knew how aiming high works. Surely, I must have discarded it because I couldn't afford it. I needed a reminder, and Gerardo, a Wharton MBA, reopened my eyes. He was the opposite of the voices around us that typically suppress our goals when we share them.

I would have to wait until the next application cycle, so I asked INCAE to defer my acceptance for one year just in case the new plan wouldn't work out. I started the straightforward research process: What are the top 15 U.S. business schools and which ones do I want to apply to given their differentiating factors and strengths? I carefully wrote the essays, and finally sent my applications. I had solid references based on my track record. I applied to what at that time were the #1 and #2 business schools and a few others. All I needed was one door to open … just one.

#1 Wharton sent me the thin "no thanks" envelope. Then, a few of them accepted me, including #2 Kellogg School of Management at Northwestern University! I literally did cartwheels in my living room after I got the congratulatory call from Kellogg. I accepted on the spot and declined further interview requests from other schools. Again, I did not have stellar undergraduate grades or GMAT test scores (both were fine, but not awesome), I did not work for a globally recognized company, and I had not climbed Kilimanjaro or done something amazing like many of my future classmates. Once again, I just showcased my determination, deep desire for more, and early career track record. And once again, the seemingly impossible door opened.

From Chocolate to the Firm

In 2010, I worked for Cadbury as an expat in São Paulo, Brazil—I will tell you in Chapter 11 how I got there, because there is another principle at play in that story. Cadbury was a loved British company that made chocolate, gum, and candy throughout the world, but in Brazil it lacked a chocolate portfolio. I co-led a top priority project for the global company's Board: The entry into the Brazilian chocolate market.

As a little kid, I aspired to work in a chocolate factory when I grew up so I could eat the chocolate as it passed in front of me in the production line!

I moved from the United States to lead the operations aspects of the project, and my colleagues Vini and Sebastian led the commercial part of the project. By operations I mean manufacturing, packaging development, purchasing, logistics, quality assurance, and even R&D in the temporary absence of an R&D leader (in other words, taking it from PowerPoint to shelf). I was having the time of my life, deeply involved in creating a new business in an environment charged with an entrepreneurial spirit, I managed multiple functional teams, we visited South Africa and India to better understand how Cadbury distributes chocolate in hot climate markets, and had a lot of fun.

A year and a half after I arrived in Brazil, and nine days before our production started, Kraft acquired Cadbury. Kraft was the absolute leader in the Brazilian chocolate market, resulting in our whole project coming to a screeching halt. After a while, I realized my expat benefits would soon disappear. I did not want to return to New Jersey since we were enjoying life in Brazil and that would have cut short the experience in an emerging economy. I wanted to experience more of Brazil.

I remembered that I certainly enjoyed my earlier management consulting experience. I cut it short only because of the attractive opportunity that Cadbury, my last client, presented to me. So, I got in touch with Kearney partners in the São Paulo office and back in the United States. They were supportive of me returning to Kearney (don't burn bridges, cliché but true). I received a highly attractive offer, and I liked the idea of returning. During the interview process though, I spoke to someone who let me know that several of his colleagues recently left to join McKinsey & Co. ("The Firm"), and suggested I speak with them before deciding. I figured more information is always appreciated to feed the decision-making process, so why not?

But wait, McKinsey, BCG, and Bain are the most prestigious strategy consulting firms in the world! Anybody in the business world knows that. Why would McKinsey hire me? I could have come up with many reasons to discourage myself from even trying, and just stick to the offer on the table. But again, I will let other people say no to me, I will not do it for them.

I went through the McKinsey interview process, was fascinated by what I heard and saw from the people I met including a few ex-Kearney, and I explained how I would add value to their clients. At this point I had the strong academics the Firm requires (Cornell and Kellogg), I am trilingual, I had a good consulting toolkit from two years at Kearney—plus a solid track record in project management, solving complex problems, and delivering value to local and global food companies.

My cell phone rang one afternoon … I got the call inviting me to join! I ended up accepting their offer, and I joined another mind-shaping journey that at times was painful but stretched me further out. As a McKinsey experienced-hire Engagement Manager, I led projects in Brazil, Chile, Colombia, Mexico, and the United States across multiple industries solving different types of business challenges. Another amazing and unexpected door opened for me, even though perhaps there were many reasons to doubt why I should set my aim to join the Firm. Something similar happened to Alex.

Alex, the Physicist

Alex was also born and raised in my hometown and went to my same elementary and high school. He thought he would follow family footsteps and started studying pharmacology at the local university. He became curious about physics during his first year, though. He then switched and became the only student in the entire country studying physics. Some classes had no books available in the library, and others had no formal professor! I'd quit at that point … the frustration must have been unbearable.

"I didn't know what a career in physics would look like, but I was curious to find out," he explained. He came to several realizations: That he would need to leave Honduras if he wanted this career to flourish and that only a bachelor's degree wouldn't cut it. He had to find a way to get into a graduate school abroad.

Upon finishing his undergrad, he applied to several master's programs in the United States but got rejected left and right despite his strong GPA because no school recognized that physics program or the professors writing his recommendations. He didn't give up. He applied to English-speaking German graduate programs, and got accepted into the University of Stuttgart, with the option to enter a PhD program if his academic records were strong. He gathered his savings of $5,000 plus a small loan and off he went.

On the first day of class, the professor gave the class a diagnostic test to assess the current knowledge level of each student. "I only wrote down my name. All the questions seemed from outer space. I had no idea what they were talking about. I cried and asked myself 'what have I done?'" Alex would start with a material disadvantage and would have to work harder than anyone. Over the next two years, he spent every single waking hour of his life focused on his studies and eventually landed a gig as a Research Assistant in a highly respected laboratory at the Max Planck Institute.

Upon completing his master's, this research group admitted Alex as a PhD student, and they moved to Berlin to establish a new collaboration between the Max Planck Institute and the Helmholtz Center Berlin (which operates a Synchrotron Facility: A particle accelerator used to produce electromagnetic radiation). Alex told me "Working within a facility of such magnitude was extraordinarily inspiring. Something unimaginable growing up in Honduras."

During Alex's four years as a PhD student, he worked even harder and learned a lot about how research projects are conceived, planned, and executed. He became wildly successful in terms of publications (the ultimate currency in scientific academia), publishing around 14 papers in the highest caliber journals. He became a recognized figure and received an invitation to do a postdoc (a two- to three-year stint where you are no longer a student, but not yet a professor) at University of California, Berkeley. He received the UC Presidential Postdoctoral Fellowship, the most prestigious fellowship given by the University of California Office of the President.

After that stint ended, he had to find a professor spot. This is where Alex's aim got wobbly temporarily: He applied to many community colleges and smaller universities, thinking he was good enough for that level. Fortunately, his mentor—a former UC Berkeley Chancellor—insisted he lift his aim and apply to the best research universities as well. "I will write recommendations for you, but only if you also apply to the best universities," his mentor told him. Alex needed a reminder.

He had six interviews with the best schools and landed six job offers. Alex is now an assistant professor at UC San Diego and Assistant Director of a massive research collaboration funded by the U.S. Department of Energy to develop a computer that works like the human brain. He's also focused on finding a room-temperature superconductor, which would revolutionize the way we store and produce energy. When discussing the value of aiming high in our podcast The Road to Champagne, he said "When you aim outside your league, obviously the best-case scenario is what you are looking for. But even if you fail at that, you learn more from a very ambitious goal than you do if your goals are less ambitious." Yes, aiming high can be a win–win proposition: You win if you get what you want, or you learn a lot in the process if you don't—which gives you more wisdom for your next attempt. And your next attempt doesn't have to be one of lower ambition. Alex mentioned; "If you go to a Plan B—a different version of your goal—it doesn't have to be lower in ambition or level. You can try another ambitious thing right after, especially if you understand what went wrong and what you could do better."

Dr. Alex Frañó, my younger cousin, kept his drive despite the uphill battles, aimed high—even if needing a reminder—and continues to grow further in his field.

Pads and a Helmet

Some people are in the camp of *not* aiming high but going for the realistic … but why make Plan B your Plan A? "Some 'experts' advise people that it is better to set no goals at all, or to set smaller, more easily achievable goals, in order to avoid guilt-driven remorse and frustration. When it comes to setting goals, the terms 'small' and 'realistic' are frequently used as synonyms."[1]

---

[1] R. Zitelmann. December 30, 2019. "Set More Ambitious Goals This New Year's Eve!" *Forbes.com.* www.forbes.com/sites/rainerzitelmann/2020/12/30/set-more-ambitious-goals-this-new-years-eve/?sh=493c943e3d00 (accessed June 2020).

I'm including a summary of this opposing view—from an article that disagrees with it—to show you this is not a slam-dunk generally accepted belief, but I would not place my money betting on such approach. If some want small results, let them aim low to be safe and take it easy.

You want to avoid getting bruised if you fail attempting that jump? Put on pads and a helmet instead of not trying the jump you've been training for! Yes, failure is part of the journey, just accept it is a possible outcome, but that should not stop you from aiming high. Woody Allen stated, "If you don't fail now and again, it's a sign you're playing it safe." Those failures will be valuable lessons for the next attempt. Aiming low is not how you will transform into the best version of You. Stick with me and believe in the power of aiming high.

Wrap-Up

So, is your aim low for a reason? Hopefully not, but if it is, find the source and neutralize its impact on you. Don't listen to the negative voices around you, which can come from coworkers, bosses, friends, family, or worse ... your own head. If you want to "be realistic" or just want to "keep it real" that is fine, but as your Plan C or safety option. Realistic is not amazing. I don't know anyone who aimed for average goals and had impressive life-changing results.

Of course, you must meet a known minimum threshold of qualification. I am not advocating for simply testing your lucky stars. I wouldn't apply to be part of the designer team at Aston Martin with my food science background despite my love for cool cars. If you don't meet the minimum requirements now, focus on building them up until you are ready to knock. That is part of the journey.

Do not wait until you check all the boxes—if you do, you are clearly not aiming high. Aiming high must be backed up by hard work, sweat, sacrifices, and discipline.

"Most people fail in life not because they aim too high and miss, but because they aim too low and hit."

—Les Brown, American motivational speaker

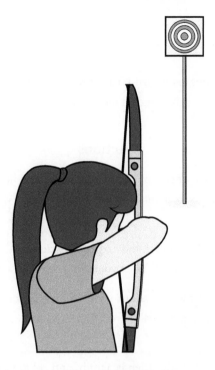

Take-Aways: Aim Outside Your League

- If you are going to aim, then aim high.
- Don't be constrained by the standards of your context, you don't always have the right voices around you when it comes to setting goals and defining educational and career ambitions.
- Don't let the prestigious aura of schools or companies or organizations intimidate you.
- Do not limit yourself: Let others try that.
- Sure, have a backup plan that is more realistic, but it should only come into play after exhausting all possibilities of achieving Plan A.

Self-Assessment

Which statement describes you best? Circle the corresponding letter.

a. I normally don't aim outside my league. I don't have those career-changing brands on my resume because I did not try.

b. I occasionally aim high, depending on the situation. Sometimes it makes sense, not always. My mindset is not calibrated to always aim high.

c. I am ambitious in my goal-setting process, aiming outside my normal zone. Aiming high energizes me and doesn't intimidate me. I go big!

Actions

- Think about where you are in your career and life and ask yourself if you're about to make a decision that will test your aim.

  o Specifically, go back to Chapter 1 Actions and review what you want more of. Does your aim need adjustment?

  o If there is room to adjust your aim, revisit your action plan to reflect bigger goals.

- Help others!

  o When you notice friends, family, and colleagues aiming for the normal outcomes, motivate them to think bigger and knock on more ambitious doors. Bring that desperately needed guidance.

  o Is anyone you care about setting their aim now?

    - _____
    - _____
    - _____
    - _____
    - _____

  o Plan what to say, how, and when:

    - _____
    - _____
    - _____
    - _____
    - _____

CHAPTER 3

Always Be WIP

I do not think much of a man who is not wiser today than he was yesterday.

—Abraham Lincoln

Why Should You?

WIP means work-in-progress, the state of a product that is not yet finished. Every food plant I've visited has WIP: Imagine warm liquid chocolate in a tank waiting for its turn to go to the molding line to become a solid chocolate bar. Once raw materials are processed and transformed, they become a finished product (a wrapped chocolate bar) ready to sit on a shelf and be sold to eager—in this case, hungry—consumers. Finished food products have expiration dates.

Being WIP means being a nonstop learner, both professionally and personally: You are not done transforming yourself, you are not a finished product yet, you are still undergoing the transformation process. It is an attitude triggered by your mindset; thus, you can control it and it does not depend on your genes, budget, age, or stage in life.

You just need to realize that to want more and aim high, you will have to acquire new knowledge or learn new skills to maximize the chances of achieving your desired next step and succeeding at it.

A McKinsey article[1] calls people who are constantly in learning mode "intentional learners," stating "While intentional learners embrace their

---

[1] L. Christensen et al. August 2020. "The most fundamental skill: Intentional learning and the career advantage." *McKinsey Accelerate.* www.mckinsey.com/featured-insights/future-of-work/the-most-fundamental-skill-intentional-learning-and-the-career-advantage (accessed September 2020).

need to learn, for them learning is not a separate stream of work or an extra effort. Instead, it is an almost unconscious, reflexive form of behavior. Each of us can become an intentional learner." The researchers go on to explain that the key ingredients are a growth mindset and a curiosity mindset. The good news, they conclude, is that these mindsets can be cultivated and developed—yes, a mindset can be reshaped as we saw in Chapter 1.

Gerald Michaelson, author of *Sun Tzu for Success* explains: "Everything on earth is either green and growing—or ripe and rotting. As long as you are green and willing to learn new things you are growing. You either get better or you get worse. You grow or decay. It's when you think you have all the answers that you are ripe and rotting."[2] When you are constantly learning, either because you have a specific goal to attain or because you just want to be more knowledgeable in a given topic, you are unleashing powerful forces that work in your favor.

I can think of at least six primary benefits of always being in learning mode, including that it:

- Increases your probability of reaching your goal (if the topic is related to your goal).
- Improves self-confidence that you can tackle unknown topics.
- Increases the probability of unseen doors opening.
- Sharpens your ability to deal with change.
- Exposes you to discover new passions, hobbies, income-generating topics, even careers.
- Ensures you are improving physically, mentally, or spiritually, depending on the topic.

Other secondary benefits exist:

- Opens new social or professional relationship networks related to that topic.
- Differentiates you from less-inclined peers.
- Brings personal satisfaction if learning is one of your motivators.

---

[2] G. Michaelson. 2003. *Sun Tzu for Success*. Adams Media.

Of course, in this age of rapid knowledge advances, it prevents you from becoming obsolete in your profession—in other words, expired.

Personally, I am always learning something or else I feel I am not taking advantage of my time and not developing myself to the fullest. For example, currently I am learning how to improve my nutrition choices through more plant-based foods, maximize rental property tax savings, conduct and edit a podcast, and improve my pool table technique. That's besides the multiple new work-related topics that always keep coming at me. Learning is now much easier for all of us: It is just a few clicks away.

Whether you reach for a book, watch videos, or pay for a class, make sure you are an intentional learner. You must always think of yourself as unfinished, still in transformation, still learning: Always expanding the breadth of your knowledge and its depth in selective areas. If you are young, you likely have a lot to learn to build expertise and be able to add value in your field. If you are older, you also must be in learning mode to avoid being replaced at work by a hungrier, savvier, cheaper version of you.

You will become stale quickly if you think you are a finished product, and you will miss out on potential exciting doors that you currently ignore. Let me share how intentional learning opened doors for me and for Lindsey.

Besouro Finds a New Home

About two-and-a-half years into my role at Cadbury in New Jersey, I completed multiple missions to help deliver value to the business. Besides the profitability improvement project for the North America candy business I mentioned in the previous chapter, I also helped redefine the manufacturing network strategy for the Americas with the involvement of my ex-employer Kearney. Plus, many other similar projects making it a truly engaging and productive phase.

However, by then I felt I had additional bandwidth that wasn't being tapped. I did not feel challenged anymore since I had my job under control; therefore, I felt mentally bored. Instead of relaxing and enjoying the peace of mind that such a state can bring, I decided I needed to learn something new to keep my brain busy. I decided to learn a new sport and a new language. Remember I told you I wanted to live in Miami? I figured if I learned Portuguese, I would increase my chances of working in Miami with a Latin American scope. I already spoke Spanish, but since Brazil is the largest economy in Latin America, Spanish wouldn't be enough. I concluded that to be a successful professional working with Latin America I would have to master three languages. That choice also influenced the selection of the sport: *Capoeira*.

Okay, I'm not sure it's a sport, but *capoeira* is a unique, intense, and engaging activity that helped me stay active and healthy. *Capoeira* is defined by britannica.com as a: "dancelike martial art of Brazil, performed to the accompaniment of call-and-response choral singing and percussive instrumental music." It also states "It was developed by slaves in the Northeast of Brazil as a disguised way to train to fight."

Wait, hold up. If you don't know what capoeira is, stop and search online for a few videos!

It is not just about learning moves that make you stronger, more flexible, and better coordinated. It is about learning the music and lyrics in Portuguese and learning to play every related instrument: A cultural immersion. Every *capoerista* (those who practice *capoeira*) gets a nickname: They called me Besouro. I hope it was in reference to Besouro Mangangá, the most famous *capoerista* who was born in Bahia, Brazil in 1885 (and not because I was one of the older guys in my class!).

By the way, during Thanksgiving that year, I bought a Playstation and exciting car games. After that long weekend, and after seeing how much of my time disappeared into a useless vortex, I realized it would prevent me from more valuable pursuits. On Monday, I gladly returned it; Believe me, I did not intend that! But I am happy I did since it was distracting me from more value-added activities. Might you have similar distractions to get rid of or better control?

Over the next 12-month period, I would go twice a week after work to a neighboring city for *capoeira* lessons and every Saturday morning

I would drive for an hour to Princeton University to meet a Brazilian tutor in a library. Eventually, I found Camila, who would come to our house sparing me the long drive. I felt I grew by learning a third language and learning a new martial art. Unexpectedly though, it went deeper than that. Guess what happened from those two voluntary Brazil-inspired learning adventures? I became extremely intrigued by Brazil: Its culture, its music, its people, and its economy. I inadvertently immersed myself in it, to the point I concluded "I want to experience Brazil. I hear a lot about BRIC (Brazil, Russia, India, China) economies having their moment (back in 2007), and New Jersey is not where I see myself. It's time to head south … way south!"

A few months later, I relocated to São Paulo, Brazil to continue to work for Cadbury, and lived there for five and a half years. My point is this: Learning will open doors you did not imagine were there. When you are not learning anything, you are keeping the invisible doors around you shut.

The World of Wines

Introduction to Wines and Spirits is one of the most memorable classes I took at Cornell. It was my first exposure to the topic. Of course, I enjoyed it because we would sample six different wines in each class, but it was much more than that. The class seriously explored the different wine regions and their varietals, terroir, regulations, production styles, and characteristics that defined those wines. I recently found my tasting notes in my parents' house from a class in November of 1993, on the wines of Bordeaux with Kevin Zraly and Robin O'Connor. Kevin was the author of the book we used in the class, *Windows on The World*. That day, we tried a 1947 Pauillac; According to the dusty tasting notes, I didn't like it. Surely that was my first exposure to aged fine wine.

Since then, I have continued to love the exploration of wines. My wine travels have taken me to vineyards in different parts of the world, usually on vacation with my wife. For my first trip outside the Finger Lakes region near Ithaca, we traveled to Napa Valley. Since then, I've loved visiting wineries in places such as South Africa, Argentina, Greece,

Chile, Italy, France, Israel, and even picking grapes during harvest at a winery in New Jersey, of all places!

Imagine sitting with a winemaker in his small vineyard, surrounded by vines, overseeing the Adriatic Sea off the coast near Split, Croatia. We talked for hours about life in Croatia during the war for independence in the 1990s, the wines we were sipping, the local culture, the Croatian football (soccer) team, and his winemaking passion. In Alsace, France, I sampled about 15 wines with the 13th generation owner of a globally known winery, immersing in their process and history. As a wine aficionado, you know wine is more than a living, evolving beverage. It is a reflection of culture, heritage, nature, science, art, and innovation. To me, being in a winery in any part of the world is a multidimensional learning experience. I am always visualizing what the next wine adventure will look like, until it materializes into a concrete vacation plan.

To feed my passion for wine knowledge, I decided to enroll in the Court of Master Sommeliers Level 1 program. It is an introductory class, the first and easiest step for any wine professional already in the business; But I was not in it yet. I had a slight disadvantage relative to classmates, but this only fueled my desire to study harder. You are expected to study theory on your own before the two-day class starts; it ends with a multiple-choice exam. Over a three-month period, I studied all 968 pages of *The Wine Bible* plus others such as *Wine Folly*, after work and during weekends. The class was fun, I learned how to properly describe the characteristics of a wine in public and how to improve at discerning a wine when blind tasting, which relies on the theory taught by the books. The person next to me came from New York, where she worked in a restaurant. She mentioned her employer would pay for the trip and class if she passed, but she would pay if she failed. Then the test results came in: I felt bad for her because she failed but thrilled that I passed.

At that time, I worked at Restaurant Brands International (RBI) in Miami, leading the Supply Chain and Procurement team for Latin America and the Caribbean, but I started the dialogue with an ex-colleague's ex-boss about potentially leaving RBI and joining their strategy team. The questions "How can I continue growing in my career? How can I make the next interesting move happen?" popped in my head again. There were several factors leading me to believe RBI wasn't the ideal long-term place for me, including the possibility of having to relocate out of the United States—I did not see myself leaving Miami prematurely after a decade-long wait to get here, especially given the proximity it gave me to my aging parents.

Southern Glazer's Wine & Spirits (SGWS) on the other hand, struck me as a place where I would also have impact, enjoy my work, and where I visualized myself thriving long term (SGWS is the 17th largest privately owned company in the United States and largest wine and spirits distributor at over $20B and growing). However, I had never worked in the wine and spirits industry. To be a compelling candidate, I believed I had to show in the interview process something more concrete than my diverse global wine travel stories. I studied for three months and I took two vacation days to attend the $525 class.

Upon completion, I sent a selfie with my postexam glass of Champagne and my new CMS Level 1 diploma to Stephen, the hiring manager I had interviewed with, saying "Cheers!" It followed a recent selfie with a famous wine critic at a wine tasting event. Months later, after I left RBI to join SGWS as Sr. Director of Strategy and Business Development, Stephen said "When you sent those pictures, I knew you were a great fit for our team and company … It demonstrated your authentic passion for what we do and was truly a differentiator compared to other similarly qualified candidates." I have been there over five years now, and I love the access to more wine training, team wine tastings, wine conferences, and meeting winemakers and wine personalities. Don't be fooled, though. My daily work (analysis, presentations, negotiations, and so on) is fun but not as exciting as those wine-related benefits of the job!

> Curiously, the more you learn about wines, the more you realize how little you actually know about such a vast body of knowledge.

If I had not voluntarily taken on the challenge to learn more about a topic that began as a personal interest, this door in my career may not have opened. Even if that door did not open, because of that small investment I chose to make, I am richer in my wine knowledge. It led to better educated decisions about wine purchases and future travel plans, educated conversation with like-minded wine aficionados, and—confirmed by author Karen MacNeil—much higher personal satisfaction: "The capacity to be thrilled by wine is ineluctably tied to understanding it in all its most basic details. Without knowledge, the soulful, satisfying part of the experience is lost." [3] I later obtained another certification from The Wine & Spirit Education Trust, Level 2.

But don't be fooled, these certifications are insignificant compared to the higher levels in these programs. I have deep respect for Master Sommeliers around the world. It's an admirable achievement that takes years of hard work and sometimes multiple attempts. You'll hear about the journey of an amazing one in Chapter 8.

Sometimes learning is not an extracurricular desire for your spare time, like my wine example. It is a must: If you don't embrace it you will pay for it dearly, as the next story explains. This happens unexpectedly in your career. Be ready to embrace learning.

Slapped by a Bear

In high school, I would get decent grades by applying a simple method: I would study the day before a test without sacrificing my beauty sleep, then show up to take the test, and get a decent B+/A– grade as a result. Simple and effective!

When I arrived at Cornell and applied this method to my first round of midterms, the results were different ... I got my butt kicked by Cornell's Big Red bear—Cornell's mascot. I mean, where would I find time to study the day before if I had classes and laboratory sessions throughout the day, every day? Introduction to Biological Sciences—a painful class—awarded me my first C– of my life! That first semester I got more Cs than As and Bs combined. Something's not right: What happened to my customary easy As and Bs? The quantity of new information thrown at me in each class surely exceeded my capacity to digest it, and I'm expected to do well in each class. It hit me: What worked back there wouldn't work here. I had to adjust and learn a new approach for this new high intensity, high pressure, fast-paced rigorous academic environment. I needed to relearn how to learn!

---

[3] K. MacNeil. 2015. *The Wine Bible*. Workman Publishing.

By interviewing and benchmarking my brilliant peers, plus trial and error, I eventually found what worked for me. A combination of these changes:

- Take good notes in class and review the notes often, not just before a test.
- Start studying for a test at least five to seven nights in advance (a night included various topics).
- Have a study partner for each class to hold each other accountable and make it more fun.
- Study in the library first to minimize distractions, then continue from my room after midnight (versus just in my room with its nice warm bed winking at me).
- Drastically shorten the amount of sleep time.

Tactically, this is how I changed my approach given the new context. And yes, the last one hurt a lot. I would sleep from 2 a.m. to 7 a.m. (plus an occasional 30-minute nap before dinner when possible), every weekday for those years. I felt so burnt out, when I went home each December, I slept 12 hours a day, every day, for those three to four weeks: My lovely mom would knock on my door to wake me up when lunch was ready.

So how did I do in my first semester with the Big Red bear slapping me around? Not well, I felt upset that my GPA did not reflect what I was used to—or my aspiration. But fast-forward to my senior year and my GPA steadily increased above my targeted 3.7 and I achieved Dean's List and became a Teaching Assistant. What changed? I redesigned my approach to studying and adopted new behaviors. But there were more consequences of this new approach. Through those adjustments, I:

- Learned how to deal with intense pressure and convert it into a motivator.
- Learned how to prioritize my efforts against competing priorities.
- Learned how to learn more effectively.
- Significantly built up my self-confidence when facing tough and unknown challenges thrown at me.

Those four long-lasting effects have shaped who I am to this day and have helped me endure many intense situations and phases in my career. They prepared me for other intense and rigorous environments, including business school and top global management consulting firms. As a bonus, my view of the Cornell experience evolved with my grades, from quasi-hate to love. I am wearing a Cornell t-shirt as I type this, one with the growling bear that welcomed me with a big back-handed slap. I now serve as a board member in Cornell's College of Agriculture and Life Sciences (CALS) Alumni Association.

When you have a challenge and the response is equal to the challenge, that's called 'success.' But once you have a new challenge, the old, once-successful response no longer works. That's why it is called a 'failure'.
—Stephen Covey, American bestselling author (1932–2012)

Lindsey Goes 0 to 60 mph

After a training event at RBI for the new incoming class of more than 50 analysts concluded, I addressed the class and explained I needed someone to volunteer 5 to 10 percent of their time to help me run analysis for a global budget I managed. Lindsey literally jumped at the opportunity on the spot—that's how I met her. After her first rotation ended, she joined my team and reported to me. Lindsey, like the rest, was green out of college, but something made her stand out: She truly exemplified what being hungry to learn is.

We began coaching the new group of Green Belts (project managers working to achieve a Lean Six Sigma certification) on how to design, plan, and execute their projects, as well as present to senior executives. The projects addressed business issues across multiple functions and were meant to provide the opportunity to demonstrate intermediate-level mastery of statistical tools. Most Green Belts took a statistics class in college or business school, but unfortunately, they never practiced it much and obviously forgot it—I can relate, and you?

I relied on Lindsey to learn the details of each project and assist each candidate to ensure their statistical analyses were properly defined, run, and interpreted. However, Lindsey studied English Literature at Harvard, and just recently learned Excel in the onboarding training. She did not fit the ideal quantitative profile for this mission.

Instead of freaking out, Lindsey realized she had a huge knowledge gap to fill and created a plan: She smartly focused on the types of analysis the projects would entail—instead of trying to become a general statistics guru—and consulted with experts to confirm if she correctly understood those analyses. Astonishingly fast, she went from 0 to 60 mph and soon provided the right advice and guidance to all the Green Belt candidates. She was thrilled to learn new skills. I had no guarantee she would accomplish the mission, but I directed her, empowered her, and let her go. She exceeded my expectations; therefore, I increased her scope.

Lindsey also became my right hand on teaching problem-solving methodology (PSM). Instead of thinking "I'll just learn the minimum to get by and please Alejandro, and then move on to the next rotation" she must have thought "How do I learn as much as possible about this because it can transform my life?" Lindsey realized that this specific skill would help her as a new professional. She saw it as the missing element in constructing a powerful critical thinking mind, and such realization converted her into a sponge thirsty for more knowledge. Despite not having a consulting background, she soon became a recognized problem solver.

I admired the way she went from ignorance to mastery of a topic and seeked more. You say "Well, she's from Harvard, of course she's like that." False, I know because she's not the only Harvard undergrad I have worked with. Lindsey's attitude differed in that she saw an opportunity to learn something new and she passionately grabbed it while remaining extremely humble and seeking for more to learn. She behaved as a WIP product.

Lindsey tried to learn and fill knowledge gaps in key topics because she realized at an early age that trying is not enough: Knowledge plus effort is required. "Without that hunger to learn from everything around and within you, there's limited opportunity for growth or exceptional performance. And once you've demonstrated that you are both eager and capable of learning quickly and taking on new challenges, more opportunities become available, which feeds the cycle of learning and experience. Those who aren't hungry to learn fall behind," she explained to me.

I enjoyed working with her because she possessed a positive attitude and saw me as someone she could learn from—I quickly perceived mentoring her would be a good investment of my time. Her capabilities grew and enabled her to conquer the challenge at hand, which meant I trusted her and gave her more responsibility. Other people in her career have also noticed that. Her statistics skills helped her get her next job in marketing at Coca-Cola. Lindsey White continued her learning quests by obtaining her MBA and joining Bain and Company as a Consultant, and will continue to thrive given this trait.

Wrap-Up

Are you a WIP or a finished product? What are you learning now? Regardless of where you are in life, you should aim to continuously learn new topics and master new skills. It is key to increasing your scope and getting doors to open: Doors you see and doors you don't. Constantly feed your curiosity by learning more about new personal and professional topics ... keep those wheels spinning up there! Do you have people in your team that are hungry to learn? Give them more responsibility and invest in their growth.

The greater our knowledge increases, the greater our ignorance unfolds.
—John F. Kennedy

Take-Aways: Always Be WIP

- Never stop learning! Always be WIP. If you think you are a finished product, you'll soon become obsolete.
- New skills open new doors. Even doors that are invisible to you now.
- If you are not learning one or two new skills at any given time, you are not investing in your future.
- Have a positive attitude toward learning. Be a knowledge sponge like Lindsey.

Self-Assessment

Which statement describes you best? Circle the corresponding letter.

a. I am not constantly learning. I am not learning anything new right now. Have you seen my schedule? I don't have time.
b. I like learning new things, but the list of things I am learning now is very short. I admit I could be learning more.
c. I am always learning multiple topics—both professionally and personally. I feel bored when I am not learning … I crave it.

Actions

- List the new skills or topics you are learning now: Are you satisfied with the list?
  - ○ _____
  - ○ _____
  - ○ _____
  - ○ _____
  - ○ _____
- If not, think about 2–3 topics you always wanted or needed to learn more about, but didn't.
  - ○ _____
  - ○ _____
  - ○ _____

- Prioritize them and write down concrete steps you can take for each topic. Create new events in your calendar to be reminded.

1. _____   <u>Target date</u>
   - _____ _____
   - _____ _____
   - _____ _____

2. _____
   - _____ _____
   - _____ _____
   - _____ _____

3. _____
   - _____ _____
   - _____ _____
   - _____ _____

- Commit to the first topic, take the first steps!

CHAPTER 4

Say Yes

It seems like the more I live, the more I realize that saying 'yes' is almost never a mistake. If you say no, it might feel safe, but then you end up going nowhere.

—Noah Emmerich, American actor and director

Why Should You?

Most of the time you knock on doors wishing they open for you. But sometimes, opportunities knock on your door. What do you do then? Every opportunity should be evaluated, but the lens we use to evaluate them vary from inclined-to-pass to inclined-to-accept. When you are inclined to accept, you are asking yourself "How can I say 'yes' to this? Is there anything critical that stops me?" But when you are inclined to pass, the question changes to "How many reasons can I come up with as to why I should pass?" which leads to a long list of excuses.

The resulting yes or no may have short-term and long-term impacts in your life, if the opportunity has any relevance (sometimes you don't know upfront). Yes is a brief yet powerful word: Like learning, it unleashes positive forces in our lives. The benefits of saying yes to a sensible opportunity or challenge that comes your way are many, including you:

- Stretch your comfort zone because you are now comfortable in more situations.
- Lose fear of uncertainty because you're now dealing with uncertain situations more often.
- Increase self-confidence because you confirm you can handle such a challenge.
- Cause doors to open in the future: Doors you aren't not even considering now.

- Grow as a professional and as a person because of the new experience you'll acquire.
- Build new relationships because of exposure to new people.

In other words, you unlock growth in your life. Growth brings positive change and puts you in a more advantaged position. Yes helps you get more: Isn't that what you are aiming for? A yes starts, changes, triggers, and stretches and it can be exciting and unpredictable. On the flipside, a no stops, maintains, prevents, and stagnates, and it is comfortable and predictable.

If saying yes is wonderful, why do many of us say no too often? Because of many reasons, including that a yes may:

- Require more effort and we are already busy
- Change our status quo and we are good as is
- Trigger feelings of fear or intimidation as we step outside our comfort zone

To maximize the chances of exciting twists and turns in your career and life, say yes to new challenges and experiences when they come to you. You have little to lose and much to gain.

Case Study Competition

When I accepted the offer to join Kellogg's MBA program, I had to come up with a plan to pay such a steep bill. Although I earned a generous salary for the Honduran context, my savings were relatively insignificant when compared to the two-year bill that I would face. I told you earlier my leadership team—rallied by Gerardo—offered to support me financially, with the understanding that I would return and continue working for them. However, the situation changed after powerful hurricane Mitch impacted the company's operations, creating revenue losses. The full scholarship changed to a loan for about 45 percent of the bill, to be paid within two years, with no obligation to return to the company. That was a kind offer: An ideal one, really, as this would open a world of career moves for me. I got a family loan for about 20 percent. But what about the other third?

Back then, if you became a summer intern (the summer between the first and second year of business school) at a top management consulting firm and they loved your performance, you would receive a full-time offer to return upon graduation from business school. Plus, payment of your second year's tuition and a nice signing bonus. Combined with the savings from the summer internship, the math now added up. That became my goal. Not just because of the financials, but because I perceived management consulting to be a post-MBA—continued business learning across multiple fields—and the type of work attracted me.

During my first few weeks at Kellogg, I was surprised to see hundreds of companies and organizations actively recruiting students to join them as summer interns, or full-time employees after graduation. It was a captivating yet time-consuming parade of companies luring us, despite the fact we had only been there for a few weeks. By the way, I still have my Enron beer glass from those events. I was also amazed by the amount of extra-curricular activities available, so I joined the Consulting Club among others.

One day, we heard that Kearney, a major global consulting firm, would be hosting a case competition where multiple teams would compete by presenting their recommendation to solve a hypothetical business situation in the auto industry. My classmates Klaus, Heng, and David were interested and asked me if I wanted to do this. But wait, the timing is not ideal as there is too much going on, I want to get good grades to impress future interviewers, I'm still settling in, this will consume precious time, I am not a consultant, and so on. But I exclaimed *"Yes!"*

These classmates were Boston Consulting Group and Accenture consultants before Kellogg—I became a sponge to learn from them and to expose myself to the consulting approach. Over the next few weeks, we interviewed mock employees at the hypothetical company (Kearney consultants playing the role of the client functional leaders), analyzed the data we obtained, interpreted and aligned on the insights, agreed on our recommendation, and packaged it into a written and verbal presentation. I contributed as much as possible—being the rookie in the team—and I learned the most. Doing this in the middle of a hectic academic quarter meant we all sacrificed sleep and free time for weeks. We won the Kellogg competition against other talented teams of classmates, then went on to win second place at the national level against winning teams from other business schools.

The outcome included deeper friendships with my teammates, winning a cash prize, and a cool framed picture of the four of us. Plus, Kearney surprised each of us with an offer to join them as summer interns, on the spot! Turns out this event was a highly sophisticated interview process that allowed Kearney (and other companies hosting similar events) to spot talent in top business schools. I later accepted the offer and successfully completed my summer internship with two fun projects that took me to Puerto Rico, London, and Amsterdam. At the end of the summer, I received the offer to join full-time after graduation, and therefore saw my financial plan materialize just as I had envisioned!

By saying yes to an unexpected challenge, I enabled the opening of the door that I needed. Had I responded "Sounds tempting but I am too busy trying to get good grades" which was true, I may not have received the top management consulting firm offer that I desired. Within about a year after graduation, I repaid the loan from my ex-employer and soon after I repaid the family loan. By the way, my concern about potentially sacrificing my GPA was overblown, since I achieved 3.8 that quarter. Even if saying yes explained the gap versus 4.0, it was so worth it.

13.1 Miles

After several years at McKinsey in São Paulo, I concluded I did not want to continue in management consulting for several reasons and I wanted to look for opportunities to return to the United States. I had two projects lined up in the United States per my request. I used Miami Beach as my weekend base, and from there I traveled to Los Angeles and Chicago for what I planned to be my last two projects, while I found an opportunity to permanently bring me to Miami.

During a Sunday morning church service in Miami Beach, a lady visiting our church for the first time, came to the front and asked: "I have a group of people running a half-marathon to raise money for villages in Africa that need running water to be installed by World Vision ... who would like to join my team? It's in three months." Crickets. More crickets. OK people, are you just going to ignore her? I felt bad for her! So, I raised my hand.

I had no idea what I just got myself into. I jogged two to four miles, that's it. I soon learned how to train for a half-marathon, and created my own plan using many online sources. It all happened during intense McKinsey projects, and became a considerable time and energy commitment. During the last month of training, Chicago dealt with the January 2014 Polar Vortex (which absolutely reinforced my need to live in tropical Miami) and I trained on a treadmill because there was no way I would go out for more than five seconds, with temperatures as low as −39°F.

Since I rapidly ramped up my distance, eventually I injured some ligaments and went to physical therapy a few weeks before the race. The first 10 miles of the race went well, but during the last three miles I had to do a slow walk-run-walk, but I accomplished the mission! It took me 2 hours and 20 minutes to finish, and my contributors helped me raise several thousand dollars for the worthy cause.

That simple yes helped transform my life: I found my latest sports passion and have completed 22 races, including 14 half-marathons since that event. Of course, I made it a challenge to improve my time, and through more strengthening and research, I am down to 1 hour and 37 minutes or 7:25 minute/mile average—not too shabby. I love running as it relaxes me while keeping me physically healthy.

Had I not replied yes to an unexpected and easy-to-ignore challenge, I might not be in the good physical condition I enjoy. After raising my hand that day, I do feel more comfortable raising my hand to unexpected challenges or proposals.

Reykjavik Here I Come

Traveling is one of my true passions. I've loved traveling to new places and discovering more about the local culture, food, customs, sights, and people, since back in the day as a little kid traveling with my parents. I have a list of 75 countries that I want to visit. I've already been to 60 countries and around 350 cities. The last country I visited before the pandemic grounded the world was Malta, after my niece Paola's wedding in Germany. Malta is a little island in the Mediterranean with a rich history and a mixture of North African, Italian, British, and other cultures. My friends and colleagues are extremely aware of this passion of mine.

Before settling somewhere for retirement, I plan to spend two years country-hopping; Living four months in a different country, experiencing life in six new countries.

One day in January at work, I ran into my friend and colleague Taylor around 4 p.m. After chatting for a minute or two he extended an invitation: "Hey, I just booked a four-day trip to Iceland in May ... you should come!" He immediately got my attention since I had not been to Iceland. I responded "Are you sure? I'll consider taking you up on the offer, send me your itinerary." I texted my wife "Is it OK if I go to Iceland with Taylor in May?" She responded "Sure." By 7 p.m. that same day, I booked the same nonstop flight as Taylor.

We rented a two-bedroom apartment and a car to drive more than 800 miles or 1200 km around the southern and western parts of the island. The spectacular natural beauty is amazingly different from the rest of the world. I've always wanted to see a glacier, and we stood on top of one at Snæfellsjökull National Park. We drove six hours each way to visit Jökulsárlón Iceberg Lagoon, where large chunks of glaciers break off, and slowly the new icebergs float their way through the lagoon to the open ocean where they end up on the beach as small ice chunks. We enjoyed the dozens of impressive waterfalls scattered everywhere, multiple lava fields, volcanoes, beaches, and geysers. I even saw my first upside-down waterfall—strong winds blow the water upwards instead of letting it fall.

In Reykjavik, we enjoyed local craft beer, a 1 a.m. jog through the city since the sky was lit, local sights, and simply exploring it. Iceland somewhat reminded me of Easter Island, although they are totally different and opposite in the map, they have commonalities: Both are a remote island with volcanoes, rich history, beautiful nature, and sit off the beaten path.

In January, I literally had no idea what I would do in May. I could have come up with at least 10 reasons in one minute to decline on the spot. But I'm delighted I did not, my mind looked for the most efficient way to say yes to an unexpected opportunity aligned with my interests. No, nothing life-changing came out of this trip, I am sharing it because the principle applies to our personal lives too! But hold on, sometimes a yes can reroute a career: If you don't believe me, ask Hector.

Hector Says Yes Twice

Hector and I grew up a couple of houses from each other, went to the same school, were huge Star Wars fans, and our families were close friends. Hector's career started as he expected, with a BS degree from Texas A&M in Agricultural Engineering which led to corporate roles in his field. After a few years, he moved to McAllen, Texas to be closer to his parents. He identified the opportunity to launch a new business: An Internet service provider (ISP) that eventually grew to over 11,000 local subscribers. With his new life as an entrepreneur going well, and noticing the housing boom around him, he also bought a franchised window treatment business (think custom blinds and drapes for a home). Everything went well for this happy entrepreneur, who later sold the ISP business to a national player.

One day, he went to the local World Birding Center to provide a quote for window treatments, during the day the center hosted an event: An exhibition by a wildlife conservation fund (The Valley Life Fund). Because the beautiful pictures in the exhibition impressed him, he asked his client about it. The client explained that the wildlife photography competition happens every two years in South Texas. Hector loved photography, a trait he inherited from his dad, but his hectic life kept him away from it. But that event inspired him to make it his new weekend hobby. So, he did!

Almost two years went by, and a few friends told him "You should participate in the upcoming wildlife photography contest!" to which he snickered, "No way, I have no time given my 8 a.m. to 10 p.m. schedule … forget it." After all, it went beyond submitting a cool picture: Participants had to create and submit a complete portfolio over a three-month period, photographing over 45 different categories of wildlife (including birds, mammals, reptiles, invertebrates, and so on). After continued insistence from his unrelenting friends, he finally replied *"OK, yes."* He put his mid-range camera to work, sacrificed a lot of personal time in this new challenge, and eventually submitted his portfolio.

Soon after, he got a call letting him know he won … first place! He didn't even go to the competition for the announcement since he was busy working and never imagined such an outcome.

His passion continued to grow. The following year, he agreed with a friend who owned a ranch to start hosting photographers in South Texas and help them take their own beautiful pictures of the local wildlife. He still worked in the window business, but his wife Liz slowly took over, which freed him up enough. As his recent hobby gradually became his focus, he started racking up accolades from competitions and magazines, making his name a recognized one. He did several solo trips around the United States to photograph different wildlife, and his local photographers eventually asked him "Hey, can we come with you next time?" Hector thought about it, responded "Yes" and took his first small group with him to New Mexico. He had to take care of logistics and event planning. It worked out well, both logistically and financially.

Let's fast forward: Liz completely took over the window business allowing Hector to dedicate full time to photography, and they eventually sold the business. Hector went on to win five more first places and two second places in that South Texas competition, plus many others of greater scope, including global competitions such as Nature's Best Windland Smith Rice International Awards (wildlife category).[1] His sessions at the ranch are now sold 18 months in advance, and he takes hundreds of people each year. His multiday photography workshops now span beyond Kenya, Costa Rica, Chile, Finland, Uganda, and the United States. He averages around 17 such trips a year. His loyal global clientele improved their photography skills by traveling with him.

I asked him how he compares his life in the successful window business versus now in photography, and he answered "It's night and day! I thought I loved the window business, but I can't believe I now have a larger income doing what I truly love! Yes, it requires a lot of effort, but I feel blessed, it doesn't feel like work." By the way, you can see Hector Astorga's work at hectorastorga.com. Do you think he's glad he chose yes twice when presented with those two opportunities? Not only did those responses dramatically change his life, they took it to a new level of bliss.

---

[1] www.hectorastorga.com

Disclaimer

I am talking about how to respond to opportunities that come to you that make sense for your career or life's growth and fulfillment: Opportunities that do not work against your priorities, goals, or values. As a strategist, I preach that strategy is knowing what you will do and what you will not do ... what is in scope and what is not. A company with a clear strategy knows what type of ventures to pursue, what customers or consumers to target, what products or services to invest in: The contrary is also true, it knows where not to focus any effort. I also stay focused on the priorities that matter. I can filter what is a low-value distraction from a value-enhancing opportunity. That prioritization ability has sharpened over time. I am not advocating for blind "yeses" from us, but for accepting opportunities that have a perceived benefit. Yes to questions such as:

- *I hear you are interested in learning more about finance, would you like to be part of this new finance project?*
- *I would like to introduce you to my friends, who like you, are also interested in practicing French. What do you say?*
- *We need someone with your skills in London, would you like to go for six months?*
- *I am volunteering a few hours next weekend to the cause we talked about, would you like to come?*

Let's say no to pointless distractions. Obviously, let's say no to any unethical, extremely dangerous, or illegal propositions you may receive, or moves where you have a high probability of failure (i.e., I would not accept a lucrative promotion in Accounting because I have no passion, interest, or skills to last long there). Finally, let's not be yes people who just agree with the boss, that is not the point. Just to clarify!

Wrap-Up

You must be open to new opportunities to grow, learn, and stretch. I love comedy, and one highly memorable Jim Carey movie is *Yes Man*. Besides being funny and entertaining, it also focuses on this principle. The result of a no is more of the same, and if you are trying to improve your career or life, practice an enthusiastic yes more often! I am extremely happy I've decided yes many times to new challenges and opportunities. We should all do it more often, like Hector did.

> *I have enjoyed life a lot more by saying yes than by sayings 'no.'*
> —Richard Branson, British self-made billionaire and author

Take-Aways: Say Yes

- No to new opportunities or challenges prolongs the status quo.
- Yes to new opportunities or challenges exposes you to new experiences, learnings, and new doors.
- Use inclined-to-accept lenses when evaluating opportunities and challenges that come your way.

Self-Assessment

Which statement describes you best? Circle the corresponding letter.

a. I don't say yes to most invitations. I have no time for new events, activities, projects, and so on. I focus on what's on hand.

b. I sometimes say yes to opportunities. The last time it happened was … hmm, a while back. OK, I should welcome more opportunities.

c. I very often say yes to invitations from others. I know it takes time, but I believe it's worth it. I welcome opportunities and embrace them.

Actions

- Be mindful and conscious of your response the next time an opportunity or challenge comes your way. Obviously assess it, but through the lens of speaking a yes (not looking for excuses to say no because you will *easily* create many).
- Specifically:
  - o Jot down a brief list of the potential attractive consequences of accepting the challenge or invitation (some are unknown yet):
    - ▪ _____
    - ▪ _____
    - ▪ _____
    - ▪ _____
    - ▪ _____
  - o Write down any **critical** reasons why you should say no (i.e., illegal, immoral, pointless distraction from a key priority, and so on):
    - ▪ _____
    - ▪ _____
  - o Identify the potential extra effort required:
    - ▪ _____
    - ▪ _____
    - ▪ _____
  - o If no critical reasons exist, are the attractive consequences worth the extra effort? _____. If so, then say yes! Remember, the positive consequences won't materialize with a no.

CHAPTER 5

Be Adaptable

Blessed are the flexible for they will not allow themselves to become bent out of shape!
—Robert Ludlum, American author (1927–2001)

Why Should You?

If you want more, aim high, continuously learn, and say yes to opportunities and challenges that come your way, you are welcoming positive changes to come and take you to a better spot. What should you do when such change arrives? You must embrace it! Change is an outcome of those steps and helps us improve, evolve, and enter a new phase. That new phase is the "more" you were aiming for. When you resist change, you are fighting to maintain the status quo which can be comfortable but doesn't lead to more. Often, saying yes requires you to adapt. When you become adaptable, not only are you prepared to deal with change, you seek it and initiate it. Having a strong sense of adaptability brings many benefits, including that it:

- Expands your professional toolkit because you are exposed to more learning curves and new experiences
- Positions you as a more effective leader because you will be better at motivating the people around you to embrace the new way
- Differentiates you as a more attractive candidate for a given mission (job, project, and so on), because flexibility has more value than rigidity

- Opens you up to more possibilities because you have less constraints when evaluating alternatives (Change industry or relocate? Why not!)
- Gives you a performance competitive edge relative to less flexible peers because they will struggle more with the change
- Brings more self-confidence and peace of mind because you know you can handle the coming change

If the benefits of being highly adaptable are clear and positive, what holds us back from embracing change? I propose there are three main reasons that hold back many:

- Change can trigger fear of what we don't fully understand.
- Change impacts the comfort of our current state, and we like comfort and coziness.
- Change requires effort.

First, when we learn that change is coming, or that it already arrived, we have no guarantees it will be positive for us. This triggers fear in many of us—that we'll lose ground and be in a worse position. Imagine you are told your current boss Mario—who likes you and even hangs out with you—was fired last night, and the new boss Daniela will join the company on Monday. For most people, this situation unlocks fear of how Daniela might negatively change the present world, triggering questions such as:

- *Will she rate me as well as Mario did?*
- *What if we don't get along like I do with Mario?*
- *Will she take away those benefits I currently enjoy?*
- *Will she change my scope, or worse ... replace me?*
- *Should I update my resume?*

Open speculative and hypothetical questions can stress many out. Many interpret the change situation through lenses that make it seem risky, threatening, and not beneficial. A survey by Leadership IQ showed 62 percent of us don't like to leave our comfort zone or do it only occasionally: "These folks are more likely to have histories and person-alities that skew their interpretation of the change more negatively." 1 In other words, their minds interpret facts about the change differently than more adaptable people, resulting in a negative outlook.

The 38 percent more adaptable people would likely ask different questions:

- *What ideas can I propose to Daniela to enable her to quickly deliver positive impact?*
- *How can I help her onboarding and increase her understanding of the political landscape to make the team more effective?*
- *What opportunities could this bring for me?*

Our interpretation filter is a product of our experiences, biases, and personalities and it affects our initial reaction to the news of change. Fear or enthusiasm.

Pause and think: How would you react to the news about Mario and Daniela?

_____

_____

Second, when we are used to doing things a certain way, we can do them with little effort. If something about our environment changes (imagine Daniela wants to optimize the department's processes, imple-ment a new expense report software she loves, and so on), we now must learn new things. Despite requiring more attention, we will be clunky at first since we will have to follow an unmastered sequence of steps, until we regain the lost efficiency through time and practice. This temporary loss of efficiency means effort is required—this frustrates many. We fall into the comfort trap of the well-known.

---

[1] M. Murphy. August 14, 2016. "The Big Reason Why Some People Are Ter-rified Of Change (While Others Love It)." *Forbes.com.* www.forbes.com/sites/ markmurphy/2016/08/14/the-big-reason-why-some-people-are-terrified-of-change-while-others-love-it/?sh=120d85392f63 (accessed June 2020).

So how can we overcome those obstacles, and learn to embrace change? Identify people around you that are more adaptable to change and learn from them (approach them and talk to them about it). Make a conscious effort to understand their point of view. Challenge yourself to apply those perspectives in your life, and little by little replace the fear with enthusiasm. Practice this in multiple change scenarios currently affecting—or soon to affect—your life. You will also see that like any other skill, the more you practice, the more natural it becomes. Soon you will feel more comfortable with uncertainty and less stressed over change. Stop yourself when you notice you are wearing negative lenses. Change happens, whether you seek it or not—learn to master adaptability.

Cultural Adaptability

One way to build your adaptability is to be exposed to different environments. If you lived in multiple countries or cities, or if you worked in different industries and companies, you surely have sharpened your adaptability skills. Those experiences forced me to think and do things differently, and to learn how to shine in each context no matter where they fell in the spectrum. Although sometimes the established culture differed from my personal preferences, I went with the flow to thrive in the new corporate culture. Of course, if you are not a good match, culturally speaking, it will be frustrating and unsustainable.

Corporate culture is a key factor that you and a potential employer need to assess, but I propose you don't need to match perfectly—a perfect match won't help you be more adaptable and won't contribute to the organization's diversity. You just need to have enough overlap to be able to operate effectively in that environment.

The more flexible and adaptable you are, the more organizations you can thrive in. Let me share a few of those cultural differences found in my journey through family-owned, private equity, partnership, and publicly traded companies of different sizes in South, Central, and North America:

- In one company, everyone understood they were empowered and were accountable for a specific deliverable, and therefore one had autonomy and made many decisions. In another, the established hierarchy meant one would have to get approval from the boss who may get approval from his or her boss before you could proceed.

- In one company, the results you achieved were what mattered at the end of the day. In another, the results mattered but also how you got them. In another, the relationships and internal network mattered most. In yet another, results, making the company a better place, and your reputation were the criteria that mattered.
- In one company, wearing tennis shoes, jeans and a t-shirt or polo was totally appropriate. In another, wearing a suit and tie plus a pocket square is the way to go when going to a meeting with executives or external partners.
- In one company, a normal and expected working day consisted of eight hours (parking lot mostly empty by 5:30 p.m.). In another company, the average was twelve hours, and if you left before that they asked you "Half-day today?" In another, 12 was a good day because the average was much higher.
- In one company, my boss gave me a hard time because I expensed two three-dollar water bottles on a business trip! He told me I should drink tap water at the hotel. I racked up points at the Holiday Inn (without drinking their tap water). In another company, at the end of a project, four of us celebrated with a lavish dinner in a fancy steakhouse, encouraged by our boss to splurge and celebrate. Holiday Inn would be inconceivable there.
- In one company, the size of your bonus was directly proportional to the percent achievement of company and personal annual objectives requiring evidence of completion, calculated with careful math. Another company used pure subjectivity.
- In one company, men and women would say good morning with a hug and kiss. In another company, HR prohibited hugs and kisses while greeting.
- In one company, efficiency mattered and impacted decision making and project timelines: Things moved fast. Each person's objectives and bonus targets were aligned across functions. In another company, dynamics of internal politics seemed to slow everything down and there were no clear incentives for cross-functional collaboration.

I could not be rigid, I had to flex as needed to be effective and not let the different approaches frustrate me or slow me down. In your profession, perhaps you deal with a different type of organization (government, academia, or your own business), but the principle holds. Be flexible and learn to adapt to a new environment. Missing how good you had it in the good old days won't help you focus and excel today. All the corporate culture changes I experienced were voluntary (I chose to leave one company to go to another), except one where the culture changed around me: When Kraft bought Cadbury. I left for other reasons, but if I would have stayed, I would have adapted and pursued success in the new context. Sometimes cultural norms change without us expecting it. Be ready to adapt quickly when needed.

I've lived in 11 cities in three countries. After the first three or four moves, I felt extremely confident in my ability to adapt to a new city and create a new social network. This of course has allowed me to pursue opportunities requiring relocation that enhance my career. Many years ago, location did not matter much. Frigid weather? Sure, sign me up! Now, I control where I live, but if I had to move a few more times to get more out of my life, I know I am capable of such adjustments.

Over 10 years ago, I flew from New Jersey to Brazil in an overnight flight to start my expat phase: I literally woke up and landed in a new country, started using my recently learned third language to get a taxi, and went to a new office to work with new colleagues in a new project related to a new topic. I searched for change, and I sure got it!

Change also boosts confidence, since you are certain you can successfully thrive in new settings after a few experiences under your belt. Remember, confidence is a key element in the virtuous cycle you must create: Want more, aim outside your league, always learn, say yes, adapt, achieve the goal, boost confidence … repeat.

Guillermo Moves Again

One of the benefits of working for leading global companies is having brilliant coworkers. One of them is Guillermo, who I met in Brazil and who ran one Miami half-marathon with me. He grew up in Colombia during the country's dark stage when cartels ruled—he even lost friends to its violence—but he kept focused and completed his bachelor's in chemical engineering, master's in logistics, and MBA. He is a great example of being adaptable not only because he worked in many organizations including Johnson & Johnson, Cadbury, Pepsico, Mondelēz, Cargill, and others, but because he has demonstrated the ability to leave an extremely comfortable life for an unknown one, in search of bigger achievements.

He was doing quite well for himself in Cadbury Colombia, when an opportunity arose in Brazil. He thought about it, analyzed it, weighed the risks, and decided to go for it (Principle 4 in action). He and his wife Maria Claudia sold their house and car in Cali, left their friends and family behind to relocate to São Paulo with their four-month-old baby to start from scratch. The right mindset allowed them to pick up and go, but unfortunately sometimes that barrier is big enough to hold back many. That's where we met, in the Cadbury office in São Paulo. Guillermo worked in the chocolate project I co-led. He worked in the procurement workstream.

Several years later, he returned to Colombia, where he and his wife were again settled in, enjoying great roles. He received an opportunity to return to São Paulo—again—for an attractive role helping consolidate five companies into one, leading the procurement function. Although they had just finished remodeling their new home in Cali, they realized an attractive opportunity knocked and they moved once again to Brazil.

This one would be his toughest cultural move, though: Going to a French family-owned company with a private equity culture. He described the culture as "Too direct, immensely controlling, highly centralized decision-making, where you weren't allowed to disagree with top executives." Not exactly what he was used to. In fact, of four executives hired for the consolidation phase, he was the only one left after seven months. He outlasted others despite the challenging culture because of his resilience and willingness to adapt to win their trust and accomplish the mission he had accepted. After he won the trust of the executives, he got the space he needed. His ability to adapt even to vastly challenging environments allowed him to succeed at his mission.

Fast forward into his career, and you find Guillermo as a senior executive in Cargill Brazil's procurement organization where he continues to grow and succeed. When asked about his sharp adaptability skills, he explained; "Attitude is critical. I am immensely thankful for the privileges and opportunities I've had, and when a new one arrives, I assess the risks and find ways to mitigate any major risks so I can proceed. I like Victor Kupper's formula that states that our value is the sum of our knowledge plus abilities multiplied by our attitude." Strong point: Attitude can magnify or minimize our value proposition. He reinforces the Chapter 1 message of wanting more but being thankful. Guillermo Rebolledo continued, "Also, I think and feel the opportunity, knowing a healthy level of excitement and anxiety is good, otherwise it is not a big enough leap. But there should be no room for fear."

Unexpected Twists

We must be especially flexible with how our career or life unfolds. We plan to go from point A to B, but we end up at point C indefinitely, or we go from A to C to B. Has that happened to you? You are not alone, this happened to me several times:

- When I lived in New Jersey, I wanted to move south to Miami Beach. I wrangled my network to try to make it happen. It didn't work. I eventually moved to Miami Beach, but only after a five-year stop in Brazil! I did not expect that enriching detour.
- When I worked at Cadbury South America, I envisioned my career continuing in the company and becoming a country manager in a small South American country, perhaps later over a bigger one. I even discussed this in career development conversations with our Business Unit (BU) president. However, after the acquisition, those plans went out the window. The BU I belonged to shrank from South America to only Brazil. Some of the leaders that supported me were replaced with strangers. Alejandro's career development wasn't a priority in that new world. Once I realized I was starting from scratch and didn't have an exciting reason to stay, I pursued plan B. That is when I returned to management consulting,

and joined McKinsey & Co. My career path took a sharp turn, but I made the best of it.

Career twists will come. If you are adaptable, they will be less shocking and disruptive. Instead of "Why did this blow happen to me? Will I recover from this?" your questions become "Where do I want to go now? How do I start moving in that direction?"

My niece Mariela, who studied at Indiana University, told me about how her career adviser asked her to draw a line between points A and B, and how she drew a straight line. Her adviser explained "Life works differently most of the time, with a twisting line that takes you to other points before arriving at point B." Very true; sometimes it takes longer to get to point B, or you go to point C first, or you end up somewhere else.

Note: It's OK to end up somewhere else, our road has unexpected turns and we can't control what's coming ahead—thus the need to be flexible. Just make sure that if you don't arrive to point B it's not because of factors under your control: Having a plan, preparing, being resilient and creative, involving others with influence, and so on.

Point A   Point B

Point C

Wrap-Up

In *Who Moved My Cheese?* author Spencer Johnson lays out a powerful story that drills into the message of being adaptable, or able to find new sources of cheese—what you appreciate in life, such as a job, income, satisfaction, relationships, and so on—when the current one is moved.[2]

---

[2] S. Johnson. 2000. *Who Moved My Cheese?* Penguin Random House.

Our cheese will move, sooner or later. Not only should we swiftly locate new cheese sources, but I would argue we should do it preemptively: Move it yourself, why wait until someone moves it under their terms? When you want more even if you are in a good place feeling blessed, you are asking for change and you are moving your own cheese. Guillermo and I have moved our cheese (triggered our next career move) at least seven times each. I am not saying you need to change jobs: Change can happen within your current organization. Change is what transforms the good current state to a great future state. Therefore, welcome change and embed adaptability and flexibility into your mindset. Adaptability is a core element of the growth mindset we need.

> *Adapt or perish, now as ever, is nature's inexorable imperative.*
> —H. G. Wells, English writer (1866–1946)

Take-Aways: Be Adaptable

- Change is inevitable if you want more. Sometimes it comes even when you don't want more. Be skilled at dealing with it.
- Adaptability can be a competitive edge in your career and life.
- Things will likely not always happen as you planned; so, be open to new paths.
- Don't wait for change, seek it!

Self-Assessment

Which statement describes you best? Circle the corresponding letter.

a. I prefer change leaves me alone, I am pretty comfortable in my routine now. Change stresses me out and causes anxiety.

b. I can deal with change when it comes. It takes some getting used to, but if/when it comes, I will handle it. Not sure I want it to come, but if it does, I'll be ready.

c. I seek change once I start feeling comfortable in my routine. Change keeps me energized and I welcome it. Hey change, where are you?

Actions

- Think of how adaptable you are: List recent examples of changes in your life and how well you coped with them.
    - _____
    - _____
    - _____

- If you relate to the group that uses a lens of fear when thinking of change, identify those around you that have a more positive outlook:
    - _____
    - _____
    - _____

- Talk to them and hear their perspectives and incorporate their points of view. What are they doing or thinking differently?
    - _____
    - _____
    - _____
    - _____
    - _____

- Invite change by talking to people who can make things happen (perhaps your boss, mentors, recruiters, leaders you want to work for, and so on) and offer to step into a new project, that international assignment, or whatever relevant change will positively impact your career. Who will you talk to?
    - _____
    - _____
    - _____

End of Part I

Notice in the diagram for Part I below the last segment of the circle is **Reach Goal, Build Confidence**. I will not dedicate a chapter to this because I view it as an outcome and not as a principle. But this outcome helps fuel the virtuous cycle: When you apply the mindset elements of wanting more, aiming high, being work-in-progress, saying yes, and being adaptable, you will start collecting victories under your belt. Victories under your belt build self-confidence. You tell yourself "I got this. Of course I can tackle this! I know I have what it takes because I have climbed similar mountains before," as well as "Now I want to climb a bigger mountain!"

Self-confidence enables you to take more risks, to speak up more often and effectively even if it is to disagree with a majority, to aspire to bigger challenges, to better market yourself, and so on. High self-confidence allows you to think "I will make this bold move because it is the right thing to do for the organization, even if it shakes the place up." The lack of self-confidence leads you to think "I can't ruffle any feathers because I'll get reprimanded!" High self-confidence makes you professionally more attractive. Just remember to stay humble, you don't want your self-confidence to cross the line and become arrogance.

> The most repulsive people I've met fell into that bucket because of their arrogance.

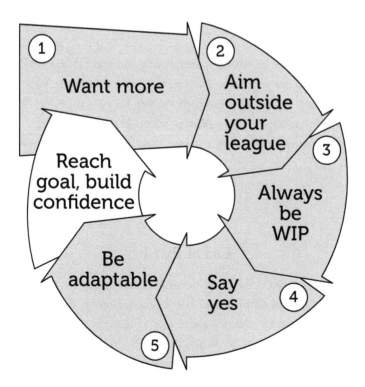

Now we have explored how to become proficient in these principles to have the right mindset for your journey. All these elements feed a virtuous cycle; now momentum is on your side.

Now let's dive into the second part of the journey, creating your professional brand.

PART II

Build Your Brand

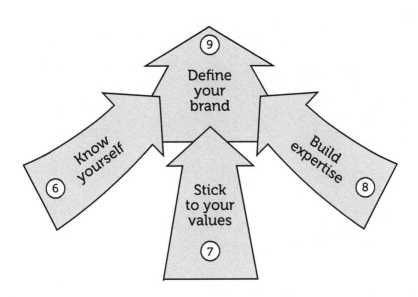

CHAPTER 6

Know Yourself

Self-awareness gives you the capacity to learn from your mistakes as well as your successes. It enables you to keep growing.
—Lawrence Bossidy, businessman and author

Why Should You?

Don't be tempted to skim through this chapter because you think your self-awareness is sharp as a razor. Hold on, I must remind us all about *illusory superiority*, the term used by psychologists to define the ultra-common phenomenon that explains why most drivers think their driving skills are above average, which is mathematically impossible. It's a distortion that leads to an overly positive view of our strengths, and a minimization of our weaknesses ... not a great combination if you prefer reality over fantasy. Self-awareness is one of those topics that easily falls into the bucket of "I'm above average ... I'm good, thanks Alejandro!" According to Harvard Business Review research, 95 percent of people think they're self-aware, but only 10 to 15 percent indeed are.[1] So, stick with me.

Having self-awareness means being consciously aware of how your feelings, emotions, and reactions are triggered by what happens around you. Why should you care about self-awareness? Because it is one of the key components of emotional intelligence (EI), a key success factor if you aspire to be an effective leader in your field—and because according to another Harvard Business Review article,[2] "Internal self-awareness is associated with higher job and relationship satisfaction, personal and

---

[1] T. Eurich. October 19, 2018. "Working with People Who Aren't Self-Aware." *Harvard Business Review*.
[2] T. Eurich. January 04, 2018. "What Self-Awareness Really Is (and How to Cultivate It)." *Harvard Business Review*.

social control, and happiness; it is negatively related to anxiety, stress, and depression." It is key to being in control of your next move, your career, and even negative emotions that can derail or sicken you: Anxiety, stress, and depression. It helps you be more effective at managing and leading a team. Without it, you won't know:

- Your anchors or blind spots (remember, this book is about removing anchors that slow our growth)
- What key relative strengths you should expand and solidify
- If key people's perceptions of you warrant corrective action or a better strategy

In other words, you're driving your car trying to get to your destination, without a compass or GPS: At best, not an efficient trip from point X to point Y, at worst you get lost and waste years. Additional benefits of having strong self-awareness include:

- Having better control of emotions when someone pushes your buttons—you can react strategically.
- Given the knowledge of your weaknesses and stressors, you can build an effective team that compliments you. Plus, you know what to delegate.
- Having better information to make career decisions.

There are two main components of self-awareness:

1. Internal awareness—how well you understand yourself
2. External awareness—how well you understand how others perceive you

Both are critical. Internal has multiple subcomponents, as pictured in Figure 6.1, the Self-Awareness Puzzle.

Self-awareness is the ability to confidently and accurately describe the elements listed in Figure 6.1. As I have matured, I have gotten much more insights about myself to be able to clearly answer those questions. But it wasn't always like that. For the first four years of my career, I did

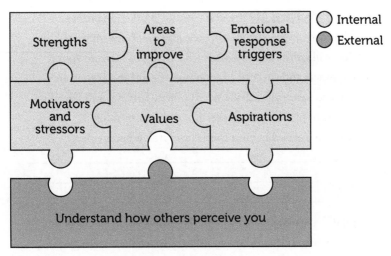

Figure 6.1 The Self-Awareness Puzzle

not do any internal awareness assessments to figure myself out. Yes, to some degree I had a good idea how to define each of the pieces in my Self-Awareness Puzzle, but I do believe self-awareness assessments helped shed light on how I am wired. Here are a few assessments I have taken between business schools and my current job, and brief key insights from them, in no particular order:

- Strengthsfinder 2.0 (now CliftonStrengths): The premise is you stand more to gain by leveraging your strengths, than by trying to improve your weaknesses. By knowing your strengths, you can seek jobs and opportunities that require or enable you to use those traits: This will better position you for success. Two of my five strengths are being Analytical and being a Learner. This matches well with management consulting and strategy, my key roles. If I shared more of my strengths and preferences, you'd understand why seeking a role in Accounting or Sales would not be a good fit for me, even though it is for others. Are you clear about your strengths? What are they?
    - _____
    - _____
    - _____

- <u>What Motivates Me</u> (by The Culture Works): Identifies
  what drives you, so you can seek jobs and opportunities
  that will constantly provide such drivers, to increase your
  happiness and success. My top five of eight motivators are
  Impact, Learning, Challenge, Problem-Solving, and Excelling.
  No surprise there, those match my choice of roles.
  Are you clear what your motivators are? What are they?

  - _____
  - _____
  - _____

- <u>DiSC</u>® personality assessment: Helps you understand better
  your work style and how to effectively relate to colleagues
  with different styles. Uses four main styles: Dominance, Influence, Steadiness, and Conscientiousness. I am a moderate CD
  which means I prefer efficiency, autonomy, logic, I have high
  expectations of myself and others, I don't easily show emotions, I don't mind conflict if it's in the way of doing the right
  thing, and I can come off as too direct. This is what the results
  say, and I must agree. It also says a stressor of mine is dealing
  with "people who don't meet your standards." True, it has
  been a watch-out area for me since I can get frustrated and
  even lose respect for colleagues who do not deliver high-quality outputs and are not making a serious effort to improve.
  Over time, this awareness has helped me be more patient
  and provide more coaching if the person wants it. More
  importantly, DiSC helps you understand the other types that
  surround you in the workplace (if they take it too), so you can
  relate and communicate more effectively with them based on
  how they are wired.
- <u>MBTI</u>® (Myers-Briggs Type Indicator®): Another personality
  assessment that helps you identify what type of work best
  satisfies your preferences assessing four dimensions: Introvert
  versus Extrovert, Sensing versus Intuition, Thinking versus
  Feeling, and Judging versus Perceiving. Imagine a continuum
  between each pair: You will know where you land in the continuum. For example, I am a moderate introvert, falling close

to the middle of the spectrum but a little toward the introvert side. This makes sense, I do enjoy time alone but also need social interactions … but too much can drain my energy. This means I need to work harder than strong extroverts to build and maintain my network, or that I get tired in a party interacting with multiple strangers nonstop for hours. I also want to point out some findings to thread consistency across assessments: "Have high standards of competence and performance—for themselves and others." "Methodical—develop detailed plans for the task at hand." Yes, I even plan out my vacations in an Excel spreadsheet day by day! How else do you expect me to know I have a train to catch at 4:15 p.m., and the address of the new hotel, what authentic restaurant to dine at, and so on? But I learned to relax and leave open time within each day to be more spontaneous, this way my wife doesn't stress out!

Are you clear about your personality type?

- o _____
- o _____
- o _____

Are you familiar with how to work with different personality types? _____

- Emotional Intelligence 2.0: Defines EI as Personal Competence (self-awareness and self-management) and Social Competence (social awareness and relationship management). If you want to improve your EI or EQ (emotional quotient), you must first be self-aware that it has room for improvement—although I am focusing this chapter on self-awareness, what you need is the whole package of EI: Understanding and managing your emotions and other people's emotions. And when you are spending 8 to 12 hours a day with other colleagues, this is a key skill for healthy relationships and effective leadership. Do you know how emotionally intelligent you are, and what you can do to improve?

I still have room to improve my self-awareness and EI; of course, they are work-in-progress (WIP). I am sharing a little of who I am, but my point is you need to know *extremely well* who you are, and the sooner you do it in life, the better. This knowledge helps you make better career and personal decisions, such as which roles and environments better position you to be successful. I found value in these assessments, and if you haven't completed any, I encourage you to explore the many options available.

A key benefit of having strong self-awareness is that it helps you make better decisions when selecting opportunities. When you clearly understand your strengths, motivators, preferences, as well as weaknesses and stressors, you can better gauge your probability of sustainable success across different opportunities. You will know project A or job A requires the skills you are great at (while exposing you to other areas you are interested in learning more about), while project B or Job B requires activities that bore you to death and you have no interest in and can cause you to fall on your face. I am not advocating you select the safest path, that is so uninspiring! I am saying you should find opportunities that will allow you to expand and leverage your strengths and will expose you to new challenges that will make you develop other needed skills you currently lack.

Don't choose a path where success is determined by mastering skills you lack and aren't interested in acquiring. For example, I recognize that a sales career in Dunder Mifflin is not for me: I would be drained because continuously interacting with uninterested buyers to convince them to buy more paper than they need while inquiring about their grandkids' kickball skills is not where I excel. I'd rather be in Dunder Mifflin's corporate strategy team finding ways to innovate as the world goes digital, assessing potential acquisition targets, and crafting new strategies for Scranton to implement. Although I would miss out on Michael Scott's madness! Know yourself, then choose accordingly.

Aggressively Seek Feedback

The external component of self-awareness is related to how well you understand how others perceive you. Dr. Jasmin Franz, a certified business coach and lecturer at the International University of Applied Sciences in Munich told me during a podcast interview, "When you want to grow in your career, you have to be conscious about your personality and your behavior. Indeed, you always want to be aware of how you are perceived by others." You must care what others think of you, especially those whose opinions influence your growth and future. Regarding your workplace, this includes your manager, other leaders, peers, and your team.

Do you know what they honestly think about you? Do they think you are as solid and great as you think you are? There's only one way to find out ... get them to share their views. Receiving formal feedback once or twice a year following HR processes is not enough. You need more frequent feedback, even on-the-spot following a specific situation. How else will you know how others view your performance in a negotiation with a customer or a presentation to an executive? Unless you are already in a proactive feedback culture, you will have to request other people's opinions. After a key meeting, I try to ask a colleague or even my boss two key questions:

- What do you think I did well?
- What do you think I should have done better?

The information you get is helpful because it points out behavior changes you should consider next time you're in that situation. Often it is as simple as "I noticed you did not make a lot of eye contact with Marie or with that part of the audience" or "The analogies you used were thought-provoking and relevant" or "Your facial expression when Dan talked made me think you thought he was crazy ... be careful." Or it could be meatier: "I thought your answer to Tony's question seemed vague and you missed an opportunity to wow them with our research findings ... you didn't seem well prepared."

There is no way around it: You need to rely on other people's perceptions of you and your performance, to identify ways to become more effective at reaching your goal. Therefore, you need to actively seek it from those around you. They likely will not offer it to you, for many potential reasons including:

- They don't think that you are interested in getting feedback from them.
- Giving unsolicited feedback is risky if the receiver is not open to it.

- It takes time: It's an investment in somebody else's growth.
- You've never given them feedback.
- They are not used to offering it.

Besides formal and spontaneous feedback, another valuable tool is 360° surveys where multiple people you work with provide anonymous feedback and ratings across multiple variables. You also rate yourself across those variables, which allows you to compare your own ratings versus their ratings of you. A tiny difference means you see yourself as they see you, and it confirms you have good self-awareness. Alternatively, big deltas point to a significant difference between other people's perceptions and your own. These blind spots must be identified to allow you to take the proper corrective measures, if needed.

I've done several, and the latest being Leadership EQ 360®, as part of a leadership program at Southern Glazer's Wine & Spirits. It's refreshing to hear all the positive feedback, and your attitude toward the not-so-positive should be one that carefully listens, filters, and decides how to act. For example, one area of improvement is that I can be too direct for certain people. Yes, I know I can because I like efficiency, transparency, and speaking my mind. I do not like sugar-coating, beating around the bush, and being too PC. For example, if I thought your idea was weak, I would want to say "Well, I think your idea is weak for these three logical reasons …" in an objective, unemotional, and respectful manner. However, since people have made observations to me pointing out some colleagues may have not felt warm and fuzzy after a direct comment like that, I constantly try to be more tactful and considerate of people who are wired differently. "Your idea is interesting, have you thought about these implications …" takes a little more effort on my part but leads to a richer dialogue and healthier relationships. I learned this by listening to others. Take advantage of 360° feedback opportunities.

When I am driving home after work listening to my hip-hop playlist, I enter a street with a 30 mph (or 48 kph) speed limit. I sense I am going at a good cruising speed, perhaps just a bit above the limit, but then I see the flashing speedometer on the side of the road flashing "Slow Down" in red. I look down at my speedometer and realize I am doing 40 mph (64 kph). I have two choices: Slow down to avoid a ticket, or ignore the signal and risk getting a ticket or causing an accident. That right there is the beauty of feedback: I am exposed to more information and a reality different from my own (which is likely biased or flawed) and it gives me information that allows me to course-correct if needed. Feedback leads to a decision on your part because you can choose to ignore it or to act on it.

I have received conflicting feedback in the past, which honestly did not lead to any action on my behalf. For example, if someone says you speak too fast when presenting and another says you speak too slow when presenting, I think you can focus on other more pressing areas.

An ex-colleague we'll call Sarah—and whose story I know is 100 percent true because she told me about it immediately after it happened and I fully trust her—had a boss we'll call Jordan to whom she never gave feedback because Jordan had not opened that door. One day, Jordan told her that she loved feedback and Sarah should feel free to give it whenever. Sarah thought about it, and decided to schedule a meeting to offer feedback.

Sarah had received feedback from Jordan multiple times before, but this would be the first time Sarah would provide it. She prepared for it in advance. As she sat in Jordan's office, Sarah first mentioned the top three things she thought Jordan did well and why she admired Jordan. She explained the professional brand that she thought Jordan represented. Then she explained how sometimes some of Jordan's actions did not support that brand. She listed clear examples of when Jordan publicly embarrassed her and other teammates, and how Jordan reacted overtly aggressively when she shared an opinion related to a business matter. She went on to explain the impact of those actions, including making her feel disrespected and less inclined to share an opinion in a team meeting. So far so good right? She started with the positives, explained how specific examples of such behavior made her feel, and why Jordan should be aware this may create unintended consequences impacting team engagement and openness.

When Jordan's turn to speak came up, the words that came out of Jordan's mouth were; "I would tell you to get the f*#$ out of my office, but I am better than that." Wow, we would expect a "Thank you for pointing that out to me, I had not noticed, I didn't mean to disrespect you. I will definitely try to prevent that, blah blah blah ...." The fact that the thought of kicking Sarah out of the office—after tactfully providing *solicited* feedback—crossed Jordan's mind, and even came out of Jordan's mouth, demonstrated that the behavior contradicted the words. Obviously, Sarah never wasted her time again giving Jordan any feedback.

If you are going to ask for feedback, be mature enough to receive it. The people giving it to you are taking risks to help you improve—be thankful. It's a cliché, but feedback indeed is a gift … don't reject it: Take it, thank the giver, process it, and only then decide how to proceed.

Here's the lesson for us: Watch out. Feedback is needed in all stages of our career. Even a CEO of a Fortune 500 company and the president of the United States need feedback. Many fall into an overconfidence trap as they mature in their careers. The higher up you go, the less you might care about feedback and your ego tricks you into thinking you are a successful professional that is doing all the right things based on your track record. But remember you are WIP, right? That means you must proactively seek feedback.

How attuned are you to how others perceive you, on a scale of one to ten? ———

It's not about you. It's about what other people think of you.
—Dr. Marshall Goldsmith, top-rated executive coach and
bestselling author

Personality Is Manageable

I've heard many times "I can't do anything about that, that is useless feedback because I can't change my personality … that is who I am!" Heard it? Said it? That may or may not be valid. If someone tells you to be less optimistic when having a business dialogue over potential scenarios, I will argue that is not good feedback. Your optimistic view must be considered and balanced with other potentially less optimistic views in the room, therefore enriching the dialogue and exposing others to views they didn't consider. And no one should ask you to be less optimistic in life.

However, if someone tells you that you are interrupting your coworkers too often by talking over them to impose your view, in a way that is not following the social norm of that work place, I would argue "that's my personality" is just an invalid excuse to dismiss what is constructive and actionable feedback. Your outgoing, bubbly, and expressive personality appears to be the reason why you frequently interrupt other people and love to dominate the conversation, preventing others from sharing their views. However, the person providing the feedback is raising very valid points to your attention: You are not allowing the views of more reserved people come up and enrich the discussion, you are making one or several of the people in the room feel disrespected, and you are building a reputation of someone who steamrolls others to dominate the airwaves. I do not buy the argument that you cannot stop interrupting people despite knowing it is having a negative impact on your coworkers.

Just like I have chosen to think twice about making a statement that can come off as being too direct, anyone can think twice about interjecting in the middle of somebody else's statement. Yes, it takes more effort, and yes it will lead to better outcomes when fixed, so work on modifying your behavior when appropriate.

Dr. Jasmin Franz from the International University of Applied Sciences in Munich explained in my podcast that our personalities are composed of our character, preferences, and behaviors: You can't really change your character, but can learn how to behave and control your emotions—especially in a business situation. Research has shown our personalities not only evolve naturally over time, but we can make conscious adjustments to negative aspects. Much has been written about it, including a Forbes article describing a five-decade long study proving that while certain personality elements remain stable over time, others change in distinct ways.[3] Therefore, personality is both relatively stable and changeable.

---

[3] D. Disalvo. August 20, 2018. "Can Personality Change or Does It Stay The Same For Life? A New Study Suggests It's A Little of Both." *Forbes.com*. www.forbes.com/sites/daviddisalvo/2018/08/20/can-personality-change-or-does-it-stay-the-same-for-life-a-new-study-says-its-a-little-of-both/?sh=5d96c1f79caa (accessed August 2020).

Remember, EI is composed of multiple aspects that include self-management: Being able to manage your behavior.

Reciprocate

Since feedback is a gift, you must know that besides seeking it, you must also give it if you are interested in the growth and success of your team, peers, and those around you. When I headed Supply Chain and Procurement for Latin America and the Caribbean at RBI, I hired two new managers into my team. They came from different industries and learned from scratch about the franchised quick-service restaurant business in dozens of countries in Latin America and the Caribbean, in a function they knew little about. But of course, I selected Ysabel and Brandon because they were bright, hungry-to-learn, high-potential young professionals. I spent the next three months closely working with them, teaching them all about how to successfully perform their roles. Topics included how to deal with difficult personalities on the other side of the phone, how this and that process worked, how to make a given decision, how to write better presentations, and so on. Every two Fridays for those three months, we would talk for 30 minutes, one on one. During the first 20 minutes I would talk about:

- What you did well these past two weeks
- What you could have done better these past two weeks

These conversations helped me discuss what behaviors I wanted them to continue (reinforce) and which ones to adjust (redirect). During the last 10 minutes, I would ask them to give me feedback using those two questions. This proved extremely helpful to all of us. "Do you need more coaching? Or do you need me to step back? How do we calibrate our dynamic?" I would ask. Then I spaced out the feedback sessions because I noticed they were well-settled into the roles and I embedded the desired team dynamic. And we did create a high-performing team with healthy, collaborative, open, fun, and effective dynamics, including Taco Tuesday happy hours at one of my favorite taco joints.

Listen to advice and accept discipline, and at the end you will be counted among the wise.

—Proverbs 19:20

Improvement Plan

Once you better understand the areas that you want or need to focus on to improve as a professional in your field, it is important to convert that knowledge into action. The best way is to create an improvement plan that includes both strengths to continue sharpening, and underdeveloped areas or weaknesses to neutralize before they become a hindrance to your growth. Create two lists of about five items each.

Strengths: Development areas:

_____   _____

_____   _____

_____   _____

_____   _____

_____   _____

Now prioritize those items based on how impactful they are to your growth, by writing next to each its rank (one through five). You can ask "If I strengthen this, will it better position me for growth and the next steps I envision? If I fix that, will I remove a potential anchor that can keep me achieving my next steps?"

After prioritizing, focus on the top one or two items on each list. Trying to deal with a long list of improvement areas at once is not the most effective way. Once you make progress on those few selected items, then you can revisit the list and tackle the next group.

Your focus will be scattered, your improvement will be slower, and there is a higher risk of abandoning the plan entirely due to the lack of tangible results.

What will the action plan look like? Keep it simple, it is just a set of concrete activities you will take in the short term to refine that skill. Be specific and add dates. Let's say you are Evelyn and you got feedback from

Wendy stating you are too quiet in meetings with key leaders or customers, and this does not promote the thought leadership brand you have the goal of building for yourself. Potential improvement plan activities include:

- By Thursday, identify the next key meeting I will attend over the next two weeks, and the topics that will be discussed.
- Research more about one or two of those topics, searching for best practices, think-tank articles, what competitors are doing, and so on.
- Select a few impactful facts, examples, or insights I want to share in that meeting.
- When we reach that topic, speak up! Plan B if needed, prompt Wendy before the meeting to ask *"Evelyn, any thoughts on this?"*
- Express key and relevant research learnings. Repeat once or twice when it makes sense to share another insight.
- Get input from Wendy soon after the meeting: *"How did I do? Should I change anything?"*
- Think about more upcoming meetings and how I should refine the aforementioned steps.

The action plan for sharpening your strengths will look similar, just a few activities you need to take to continue learning more about that topic, showcasing that expertise, and applying it further to enhance the results of your team.

I did my first thorough improvement plan about 15 years ago, when I worked with Pat, a leadership coach, to achieve my goal of being a more effective leader and better defining my career path. In it we defined potential future roles and key skills I needed to get me there. It was a valuable exercise and tool at that time in my career.

Now, write down concrete actions for the top one or two areas, including completion dates:

Target date:

Strength #1: _____

Actions: _____   _____
            _____   _____

_____   _____

_____   _____

Strength #2: _____

Actions: _____   _____

_____   _____

_____   _____

_____   _____

Development area #1: _____

Actions: _____   _____

_____   _____

_____   _____

_____   _____

Development area #2: _____

Actions: _____   _____

_____   _____

_____   _____

_____   _____

Our goals can only be reached through a vehicle of a plan, in which we must fervently believe, and upon which we must vigorously act. There is no other route to success.

—Pablo Picasso, Spanish artist and painter (1881–1973)

Wrap-Up

There are many great sources of deeper information about self-awareness and EI that I motivate you to explore, including books, online resources, and courses. Consider this chapter a high-level overview with the aim of emphasizing how critical this is to your mindset and growth journey. Take action to know yourself well and understand how you are perceived (especially by those around you who can influence your growth).

Know the enemy and know yourself, and you can fight a hundred battles with no danger of defeat. If ignorant both of your enemy and yourself, you are sure to be defeated in every battle.

—Sun Tzu, Chinese general and writer (circa 500 BC)

Take-Aways: Know Yourself

- Emotional intelligence (EI) is crucial to become an effective leader. It can be increased by exploring, assessing, and working on your:
  - Personal competence
    - Internal self-awareness
    - External self-awareness
    - Self-management
  - Social competence
    - Social awareness
    - Relationship management
- You must be in tune with how others perceive you. This is achieved by proactively seeking feedback.
- Carefully listen to, process, and filter the feedback you receive. If relevant and actionable, create an improvement plan.
- Invest in others' growth by giving them feedback.

Self-Assessment

Which statement describes you best? Circle the corresponding letter.

a. I can describe certain internal components of self-awareness, but I stumble on some. I am not confident I truly understand how others perceive me.

b. I can accurately describe most of my internal components of self-awareness. My understanding of how others perceive me is something I need to improve.

c. I can accurately describe all my internal components of self-awareness. I understand well how others perceive me. Feedback is my friend.

Actions

- If needed, explore which available self-awareness assessments and EI assessments attract you and consider completing some. List them here:

  Assessment type: Options:

  _____   _____

  _____   _____

  _____   _____

  _____   _____

  _____   _____

- After exploring the options, circle above the assessment(s) you will complete.

- Create two lists: One of people to request objective feedback from, another you will offer feedback to (confirm they are interested). Talk to them and get the ball rolling!

  I will give feedback to: I will request feedback from:

  _____   _____

  _____   _____

  _____   _____

  _____   _____

  _____   _____

- If you have not done it already, develop an improvement plan to refine your strengths even more, and to address any weaker areas highlighted by the feedback sessions.

CHAPTER 7

Stick to Your Values

Values are like fingerprints. Nobody's are the same but you leave them all over everything you do.
> —Elvis Presley, American singer and actor (1935–1977)

Why Should You?

Notice that in the previous chapter, I listed values as one of the key elements of self-awareness, but we didn't go into it. That is because values warrant their own standalone chapter and principle.

Your values are a set of ingrained beliefs that you hold as guiding principles. They help define your judgment and character and help you navigate life's decisions. Your values and my values have been defined by our context, upbringing, experiences, and influences. Every individual has a set of values. An individual may or may not be able to effectively express what those values are and may or may not live according to those values.

Even organizations or companies have them, including your employer or the ancient samurai with their Bushido Code. Corporate values help constituents understand which behaviors are admired and which are shunned; therefore, calibrating mindsets, behaviors, and actions.

My values are different from yours, which are different from your cousin's. We all have a different set of values because there are many options to build a value set from. The list of options varies depending on the source. According to mindtools.com[1] for example, personal values include:

---

[1] Reproduced with permission from MindTools.com. 2020. *What Are Your Values?* [Online]. Available from: www.mindtools.com/community/pages/article/new-TED_85.htm. (accessed June 2020).

Accountability	Discipline	Humility
Accuracy	Discretion	Independence
Achievement	Diversity	Ingenuity
Adventurousness	Dynamism	Inner Harmony
Altruism	Economy	Inquisitiveness
Ambition	Effectiveness	Insightfulness
Assertiveness	Efficiency	Intelligence
Balance	Elegance	Intellectual Status
Being the best	Empathy	Intuition
Belonging	Enjoyment	Joy
Boldness	Enthusiasm	Justice
Calmness	Equality	Leadership
Carefulness	Excellence	Legacy
Challenge	Excitement	Love
Cheerfulness	Expertise	Loyalty
Clear-mindedness	Exploration	Making a difference
Commitment	Expressiveness	Mastery
Community	Fairness	Merit
Compassion	Faith	Obedience
Competitiveness	Family-orientedness	Openness
Consistency	Fidelity	Order
Contentment	Fitness	Originality
Continuous	Fluency	Patriotism
Improvement	Focus	Perfection
Contribution	Freedom	Piety
Control	Fun	Positivity
Cooperation	Generosity	Practicality
Correctness	Goodness	Preparedness
Courtesy	Grace	Professionalism
Creativity	Growth	Prudence
Curiosity	Happiness	Quality-orientation
Decisiveness	Hard Work	Reliability
Democraticness	Health	Resourcefulness
Dependability	Helping Society	Restraint
Determination	Holiness	Results-oriented
Devoutness	Honesty	Rigor
Diligence	Honor	Security

Self-actualization	Stability	Tolerance
Self-control	Strategic	Traditionalism
Selflessness	Strength	Trustworthiness
Self-reliance	Structure	Truth-seeking
Sensitivity	Success	Understanding
Serenity	Support	Uniqueness
Service	Teamwork	Unity
Shrewdness	Temperance	Usefulness
Simplicity	Thankfulness	Vision
Soundness	Thoroughness	Vitality
Speed	Thoughtfulness	
Spontaneity	Timeliness	

Each of these has an impact on you, ranging from insignificant to massive. Now you understand why Elvis illustrated them as fingerprints: There are many variables at play leading to different people having different value sets. Looking at this list, reflect on your values and circle the ones that resonate (circle twice those you consider stronger or core to you). Then, for cleanliness, write down which values are part of your values set:

Core values: _____, _____, _____

_____, _____, _____

Others values: _____, _____, _____

_____, _____, _____

_____, _____, _____

Just like with other aspects of self-awareness, you will benefit from clearly understanding what your value set is. Your values are like a compass that helps point you in the right direction; a direction that gives you inner peace and satisfaction when followed in your career and life. But when you don't truly understand your values, it is more difficult to understand the right direction to pursue. Option A or B or C? There are multiple benefits that arise from being in-tune with your values, including:

- *Making the best decisions for your career and life.* Key decisions are best taken when they are aligned with your values. For example, what career should I choose? Who should I marry?

Should I go for that new opportunity? The consequences of misaligned critical decisions can include years of dissatisfaction and regret.

- *Prioritizing between competing choices.* Sometimes you are pulled in multiple directions simultaneously and you must choose. For example, next Wednesday should you attend that key meeting your boss expects you to lead in Atlanta, or attend your daughter's fifth birthday party back home in Chicago? Sometimes you consciously alternate what to sacrifice or get creative to minimize downsides.

- *Selecting a position or stance in an issue.* Simple choices are governed by your value set. For example, your stance regarding recycling practices, immigration policies, exercise and diet, gun policies, and so on. On all issues, you fall somewhere in the continuum, and that position is influenced or governed by what you value more.

- *Understanding your best possible action when facing a difficult situation.* Within a specific situation, you have choices. For example, you hear a guy verbally abusing a lady at your local coffee shop. Do you ignore it, confront him, leave, or ask the manager to get him out? How you react is also influenced by your values. Sometimes the situation is less public: What do you do if your boss asks you to change the analysis result, to avoid contradicting his recommendation?

- *Confirmation that your actions were appropriate.* After you made a choice and acted upon it, you will have to live with the consequences. Is the consequence a feeling of satisfaction and peace or of frustration and shame? Your values help you confirm if you took the best course of action: The one that is aligned with how you should behave given your value set.

All those benefits are important and relevant, and they will come into play in different moments of your life. I think values are like your trusted brands, they help the decision-making process be efficient. For example, if you are loyal to a brand such as Nike, the next time you need running shoes you will go check out Nike's running shoes and pick one from those options. You are not going to start from scratch and explore all the options in the product portfolio of New Balance, Reebok, Saucony, and so on. Because I like fine chocolate brands such as Valrhona, Vosges, and Neuhaus, I will ignore all the mass market brands like Hershey's or Snickers competing for my attention in the chocolate aisle. Like brands, values help eliminate potential choices when you realize they are not well-aligned with who you are, and they help you identify the best choice.

Do you understand your values with precision? I bet that you already know most of your key values. Perhaps you may not be able to immediately describe the pecking order of these values. Which ones are more important to you? To understand your values, you can rely on available online assessments like the ones that gauge your self-awareness, but a good self-introspection with pen and paper or keyboard can do the trick, too.

According to a recent values assessment I did, my stronger values include ethics/morals, spirituality, hard work/diligence, power/influence, competitiveness, knowledge, intellectualism, and empathy. It did not surprise me much. Let's explore how values play out in our behavior, decisions, and actions.

Diversity

Diversity is another value of mine, although it did not come up in such assessment. One of the many ways that Cornell University enriched my life includes exposing me for the first time to real diversity. Before Cornell, I was in a homogeneous environment in my hometown in Honduras. I was later in a totally different world and I loved it. Now I had friends from Morocco, Poland, Barbados, Ecuador, and so on, plus every corner of the United States. My roommates and apartment mates were diverse, including students from Japan, Venezuela, plus several states. During my sophomore year, I shared a cool apartment with a high-rise view of the campus with Evan, Derek, and Ed—all from different races and backgrounds. It was my new normal.

Throughout Cornell, I found diversity of background, economic status, extracurricular activity interests, sexual orientation, academic pursuits, world views … you name it. It was eye-opening. It also exposed me to segregation I ignored. For example, some dorms, fraternity houses, student associations, even Bible study groups were primarily for one racial or ethnic group. I am sure it's based on students' preferences, but that was new to me: I would have expected everyone to blend and mix naturally.

Returning to Honduras after graduation created a big cultural shock for many reasons, including going back to limited diversity. Eventually, I returned to a similar diverse environment at business school.

Different shades of skin color are awesome and needed, but even better is diversity of thought. In my sophomore apartment example, our different backgrounds, values, majors, goals, personalities, and hobbies brought even more diversity—beyond the fact that we looked different from each other. In a work environment, that diversity of thought leads to richer outcomes. People trained in one field are, by definition, not trained in other fields; therefore, they have limited range of sight into all issues. Creating an environment where different views come together results in an enriched conversation and outcome.

Katherine W. Phillips, who was a Columbia Business School and Kellogg professor, explained it well: "The fact is that if you want to build teams or organizations capable of innovating, you need diversity. Diversity enhances creativity. It encourages the search for novel information and perspectives, leading to better decision making and problem solving. Diversity can improve the bottom line of companies and lead to unfettered discoveries and breakthrough innovations. Even simply being exposed to diversity can change the way you think."[2] Deloitte also explains the associated benefits of diversity of thoughts to an organization or team, including helping guard against groupthink and increasing the scale of new insights.[3]

A 2019 McKinsey study concluded that companies in the top quartile for *gender* diversity on executive teams were 25 percent more likely to have above-average profitability than companies in the fourth quartile.

[2] K.W. Phillips. September 18, 2017. "How Diversity Makes Us Smarter." *Greater Good Magazine*, https://greatergood.berkeley.edu/article/item/how_diversity_makes_us_smarter (accessed May 2020).

[3] A. Diaz-Uda, C. Medina, and B. Schill. July 24, 2013. "Diversity's New Frontier." *Deloitte Insights*.

The likelihood changed to 36 percent for *ethnic* diversity.[4] It also points out that it is not just about hiring diversity, it is about ensuring a work environment "characterized by inclusive leadership and accountability among managers, equality and fairness of opportunity, and openness and freedom from bias and discrimination." Otherwise the benefits of diversity are hampered.

I have also been fortunate to work in work environments in the United States and Brazil that foster diversity. I value diversity to the point that I have not considered job opportunities after noticing a very homogenous group during the interview process. I also would not live in a city or neighborhood or that does not represent the diversity I've grown to appreciate. I enjoy hearing multiple languages when I walk through my neighborhood. Diversity of gender, ethnicity, and of thought do matter.

This value led me to propose an answer to a companywide competition aimed at answering "how can we achieve our diversity and inclusion vision?" in a 20,000+ employee organization. Out of 500+ ideas, 11 were selected to present to 10 executives in a "Shark-Tank" fashion, and they recognized my idea as the winner: I used my problem-solving and influence skills to get it implemented, and now senior leaders have diversity and inclusion metrics tied to their bonus so they have a hard motive to care about it and promote it. I gladly spent many hours researching, benchmarking, interviewing, and building a thorough business case to effectively increase diversity (starting with the top team)—because I care about it.

Dissent

One of the things that I learned early on after joining McKinsey & Co. is that the set of 15 values is taken seriously. In many companies, values are aspirational because they are not yet lived, in others they are just a nice decoration on the wall. One of the McKinsey values that I continue to

---

[4] V. Hunt, S. Prince, S. Dixon-Fyle, and K. Dolan. May 19, 2020. "Diversity wins: How inclusion matters." *McKinsey & Co.* www.mckinsey.com/featured-insights/diversity-and-inclusion/diversity-wins-how-inclusion-matters (accessed August 2020).

live, even after leaving years ago, is: "Uphold the obligation to dissent." When a CEO or executive hires McKinsey to help answer a strategic question, and pays top dollar for such services, the last thing she (or he) wants is a bunch of yes people who simply will tell her what they think she wants to hear. By telling its consultants that they have the right to dissent and are expected to do so, The Firm is requesting its consultants express their views even if contradictory to the position of the key senior client team or the rest of the McKinsey team. It is empowering its consultants and demanding that different views are brought to the table.

Why? The Firm realizes that such dynamic enriches the conversation by exposing views, risks, or implications that may not have been considered. Therefore, the probability of arriving at the optimal solution is increased.

This belief is confirmed by author Charlan Nemeth, who explains that "Consensus, while comforting and harmonious as well as efficient, often leads us to make bad decisions. Dissent, while often annoying, is precisely the challenge that we need to reassess our own views and make better choices. It helps us consider alternatives and generate creative solutions. Dissent is liberator."[5] He goes on to explain that when confronted by dissent we are more likely to consider pros and cons and arrive at more creative solutions. On the flip side, it can slow decision making and increase team conflict. He concludes that overall, dissent leads to positive outcomes even if the dissenting position turns out to be wrong, because it opens the team to be more fact-based and prone to learning.

I currently work in an environment where I can freely practice this value, and my team and manager now fully expect this of me. I have enough experience to gauge the attractiveness of the choices ahead and I'm confident enough to voice my opinions (isn't someone paying me to think?). I am not shy about proposing alternative views, constructively questioning others' logic, and expressing my disagreement in private or in public. I do this because I care about my teams' work and the company's results: I want to ensure that we're taking the best path possible given the information at hand.

---

[5] C.J. Nemeth. 2018. *In Defense of Troublemakers–The Power of Dissent in Life and Business*. Hachette Book Group.

My input can end up being the best one and it will redirect the decision or be totally off and I will learn more about the validity of the prevailing thought. I must know when to back off, though, otherwise I would go from a solid thought partner to a pushy opposer. My views may not always be influential, but that's part of the process.

Just a word of caution before you decide to give authentic bold dissent a try in your upcoming meeting. The degree of tolerance for dissent varies based on the culture of your organization. Understand that context before putting yourself in such a situation. According to an article in *The Economist*,[6] "The ability to speak up within an organization, without fear of sanction, is known as 'psychological safety.'" It goes on to explain how a study concluded that self-reported psychological safety was by far the most important factor behind successful teamwork at Google. Not every organization will be as mature as Google or McKinsey when it comes to psychological safety; so, know your context but do try to influence it. I brought this value with me and I have actively used it in a context not as open as Google or McKinsey. I did have to educate others by explicitly explaining the benefits of dissent, to get them used to it. It is a tool I constantly use to add value.

We owe almost all our knowledge not to those who have agreed but to those who have differed.
—Charles Caleb Colton, British cleric and writer (1780–1832)

Hard Work and Excellence

I have always strived to be great at the task at hand. I may not the best for the mission, but I will wrestle with it, learn rapidly, work hard, then deliver an outcome that meets or exceeds expectations. Hard work + effort to learn + perseverance is a true and tested recipe for success. If I were naturally amazing, I could do things effortlessly, but I am not ...

---

[6] Bartleby. October 10, 2019. "In Praise of Dissenters." *The Economist*. www .economist.com/business/2019/10/10/in-praise-of-dissenters (accessed June 2020).

hard work is required! Mark Cuban stated, "It's not about money or connections—it's the willingness to outwork and outlearn everyone."

Sometimes hard work meant starting my Monday at 2:30 a.m.! I feel tired just remembering that. When I led the Quality Assurance (QA) department at the shrimp farms' main processing plant, the senior members of the corporate QA team would rotate and do daily preproduction inspections at the plant using protein-detecting rapid tests to ensure all the production lines were properly sanitized and ready for another day of production. We did this at 5 a.m. Sometimes, my duty fell on a Monday. Many times, I happened to be two hours away at my parent's house in the capital city spending the weekend. I would have to leave by 3 a.m. I wouldn't let my team down by not sticking to my commitment.

Sometimes hard work meant sacrificing sleep and food. Experienced hires at McKinsey typically do not lead their first project, they take a role one level below to learn more about the McKinsey way before leading a client project. During the first few weeks of my first project, we left the client site and went to continue working at a table in the hotel lobby. I was starving … it was around 9 or 10 p.m. The team kept cranking away at their laptops, all working on parts of a presentation for a review the next day. I told the project manager "Hey man, we should order dinner" and he mumbled "Yeah, soon." We kept discussing work, typing away, making slides.

Repeat the last two sentences a few times. It's 1 a.m. Still, no one talked about dinner. What?! I had never skipped dinner in my entire life! I did not want to be the weak link breaking away from the team in a time of focus, and these guys somehow learned to ignore hunger. We stopped after 3 a.m. I felt exhausted and went straight to bed at 3:30 a.m. and woke up at 7:00 a.m. to start a new day. That dinner-less long night reminds me I *can* push myself to accomplish what needs to be accomplished (it also reminds me to be empathic toward my team: Everyone should be well fed and energized for such a task … basic EI stuff).

I make the necessary effort to meet or exceed expectations and avoid sloppy or half-baked outputs. My mom ingrained high standards as a value in me as a little kid, and this sometimes means making many small sacrifices.

I do not know anyone who has got to the top without hard work. That is the recipe. It will not always get you to the top, but should get you pretty near.
    —Margaret Thatcher, British prime minister (1925–2013)

Generosity

Since being a little girl, Rissa spent summer and Christmas vacations in Jamaica, where part of her family lives. For such trips, her parents would bring extra bags of clothes to donate. Rissa visited orphanages and schools on the island and handed it out to the kids. Also, her grand aunt Grace, a retired teacher who worked at one of the best high schools in the island, would take Rissa with her to show her the value of education and how it helps change kids' lives. The values of generosity and education started to form in her value set given her childhood experiences and consistent family examples.

Her Harvard Business School's class commencement speech, given by Ken Chennault, former CEO of American Express, vigorously reinforced the value of generosity—and it stuck with her. She says "I clearly recall him reinforcing the need to give back no matter how successful we are: Even more if we become highly successful. That speech strongly influenced me." She eventually joined American Express after a few years at Goldman Sachs, and she witnessed how a company can actively give back and how individuals enthusiastically took advantage of such opportunities. The company offered many volunteering initiatives to its employees, including food drives, soup kitchens, and others. She chose to volunteer helping build houses for underprivileged members of the local community.

The combination of her value of generosity plus the appreciation of how education improves lives, led her to action. She launched Grace Scholarship Fund (GSF) to help Jamaican high school students with high potential and academic performance pay for local colleges and universities. Many parents of bright students can't afford to invest in their next educational goal. GSF became an international effort with global supporters. Since inception, GSF has awarded 50 scholarships to students from across the island.[7]

---

[7] www.gracefund.org

At Southern Glazer's Wine & Spirits, my coworker and friend Rissa Lawrence continued her active participation in initiatives to help give back to others, including co-developing a comprehensive executive education experience for women in our organization and co-designing and deploying Diversity & Inclusion (D&I) roadshows to educate thousands of employees on relevant D&I topics. She also enjoys mentoring a minority college intern. "I expect the company I work for to have a similar focus on giving back," she explains, "or else I would not be a great fit."

Spirituality, Integrity, Respect

Remember, each person has different values, and just like I don't expect you to have my same values, you don't expect me to have yours. I am saying it to shed light on how this core value impacts my life, just like other values impact your life. My Christian upbringing meant going to church, reading the Bible, praying, and so forth. Since early on, I have prioritized my relationship with God. That translates to multiple day-to-day actions and choices such as being thankful, having integrity of character, and respecting others, for instance.

Integrity is about knowing what is right, striving for it, and when failing, admitting it and course correcting. Integrity is about not cheating on your exam, expense report, or tax return. It's about not taking advantage of others even if you could get away with it. It's about doing what you say you will do: Keeping a secret when someone confides in you or showing up when you said you would. Integrity is a value I learned from my parents.

One of my many bosses once asked me to change the results of an analysis to increase the chances of passing an external audit critical to enter a new market. I refused, and instead prepared logical explanations for such results and an improvement plan to demonstrate we knew how to fix it. The auditors were impressed with the self-awareness and proactiveness shown about the deficient KPI and we passed the audit. I felt proud of myself for sticking to my values, and I confirmed I do not need to succumb to such pressure in future similar situations. Homey don't play that!

I believe everyone has the right to be treated with respect, independent of the size of their bank account, color of skin, or intellectual prowess. Why? To me it's because God created us as equals and asks us to love our neighbors and show compassion. All of us will agree that we like being respected; however, we don't always respect others. When I witness someone being disrespected or someone disrespects me, my blood heats up. I have worked and dealt with a wide range of people, from unskilled laborers in shrimp farms in the south of Honduras, to CEOs of successful global companies. I treat them the same, with courtesy and respect. It's not hard at all! Looking down at people is a huge mistake! One could lose followership, a term commonly used at McKinsey to describe others' desire to work for you and be around you. Lack of followership is failed leadership, independent of the title you achieved.

Prioritization

You may think that my career is the top priority in my life based on the experiences I have shared throughout this book—and the topic of the book. No, it lands fourth in my pecking order. Yes, if urgent, I'll choose to skip a Bible study or family dinner to finish a key business deliverable due tomorrow morning, because the pecking order has flexibility depending on the circumstances. I would not sacrifice my health for a promotion, but three days ago I skipped my workout because I had to work later than usual: There are small give and takes frequently happening to achieve the best overall outcome, it is not a rigid system.

Wrap-Up

Being conscious of the ranking of your priorities and values makes you aware of trade-offs and sacrifices needed, allowing you to keep track and gauge if your overall actions are consistent with your stated priorities and values. It leads you to make necessary changes. Bring those values to life, as Rissa did with the launching of her education scholarship fund, and let them shine as part of your professional brand.

It's not hard to make decisions when you know what your values are.
—Roy Disney, American businessman (1893–1971)

Take-Aways: Stick to Your Values

- Values are a critical element of self-awareness; therefore, you need to be clear what your values are.
- Use your values to help you make the best career and life decisions and to gauge if your behaviors are consistent with who you truly are.

Self-Assessment

Which statement describes you best? Circle the corresponding letter.

a. I have some general idea what my values are, but I would have to think if asked about them. I am not sure I can tell you off the top of my head how I prioritize them.

b. I can describe most of my core and secondary values. I know their prioritization: I have a couple of examples of how I used that to make career, life, and day-to-day decisions.

c. I can accurately describe my core values and my secondary values. I know how I prioritize those values and I always refer to them to make career, life, and day-to-day decisions.

Actions

- Get clarity on your core values and secondary values either by doing an assessment or by introspection:
  - o Explore assessment alternatives, or
  - o Use the values listed earlier and circle the ones that resonate (circle twice the core ones) if you haven't done so
- Look for proof. Think of ways you have let your values guide your steps.

_____

_____

_____

- Think about any necessary changes you should consider, given your value set.
  - o Are there things you need to do more of?
    - ▪ _____
    - ▪ _____
    - ▪ _____
    - ▪ _____
  - o Are there things you need to do less of?
    - ▪ _____
    - ▪ _____
    - ▪ _____
    - ▪ _____

CHAPTER 8

Build Expertise

True expertise is the most potent form of authority.
—Victoria Bond, American conductor and composer

Why Should You?

Now that you know yourself better, including your strengths, interests, motivators, and values, you are better positioned to build serious expertise. You want to be known for at least one thing you do much better than others (and several you do equally well to be well-rounded). This is how you differentiate yourself from the pack

What pack? Any group with similar credentials and skills as you trying to achieve the same goal: Your classmates interviewing with the same companies as you, your colleagues competing for the same exciting assignment or promotion, or if an entrepreneur, the other business owners your potential clients can select instead of you.

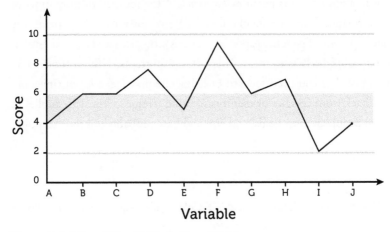

Figure 8.1 Plot of Key Skills in Your Field

That superior performance or deep expertise in a topic is referred to as a *spike* because if you graphed your performance across multiple variables, as shown in Figure 8.1, visually you would be way above the average. Let's imagine that we were to select 10 variables that matter to excel in your field, and then score you in each one as shown in the Figure 8.1.

As you can see, there are a few insights to extract from the following figure:

- Awesome news: You have a significant spike in variable F
- Great news: You have smaller yet compelling spikes in D and H
- Bad news: Your performance in variable I needs improvement
- Your performance across the other key variables is average (scores of 4–6)

When you differentiate yourself through one or two spikes, you increase demand for your services. When you increase demand for your services, doors open in the shape of appealing proposals, job offers, cool projects, promotions, invitations, referrals, and so on. A chef can become successful and famous without having to cook every imaginable dish to perfection; they can excel at one segment of gastronomy to achieve that, perhaps chocolate pastries or fine Vietnamese. Key word: *Excel*. In my field, I don't need to be the go-to person for every business topic affecting the food and beverage industry, obviously. Excelling in just a few will suffice.

Building a spike to distinguish yourself takes time and effort. According to a Harvard Business Review article, "The journey to truly superior performance is neither for the faint of heart nor for the impatient. The development of genuine expertise requires struggle, sacrifice, and honest, often painful self-assessment. There are no shortcuts."[1] The authors go on to argue that you need focused or deliberate practice, a lot of time, and feedback from coaches or mentors to build strong spikes. This applies to most people in most fields, and you and I are probably not the exception.

---

[1] K.A. Ericsson, M.J. Prietula, and E.T. Cokely. July–August 2007. "The Making of an Expert." *Harvard Business Review*.

Perhaps you have already built them, or you still need to build them. Regardless of where you are in that construction journey, know that this is key to your professional success and brand. Even after building a spike, you need to maintain it. Spikes that are not well-maintained will shrink over time as the world and the topic of your expertise continue to evolve and/or your peers proactively improve. That is why that article describes superior performance as not for "the faint of heart nor for the impatient."

The Main Spike

The main spike is that one variable you really shine at—where you have depth in expertise. If you have two, that's awesome, but you need at least one recognized main spike. I've mentioned problem-solving multiple times because it's my main spike. Problem-solving is finding the optimal solution to a given opportunity or complex challenge to close the gap between the current state and the desired state. We are here in spot X but need or want to be in spot Y: The gap to close between X and Y is referred to as a problem. Problems can afflict a person, group, organization, or country (or a continent, or planet ... you get it). Solving a problem creates value. Problem-solving methodology (PSM) is a structured, logical method for solving any type of problem.

This book is a product of applying PSM to the problem: "Why are most professionals *here* when they have the potential to be *there?*" By "there" I mean farther ahead in our career. And I say "our" not "your" because I am including myself ... such problem has affected me too, which allows me to understand and see the problem from the outside as a problem solver and from the inside as someone who has lived it.

We can apply PSM to situations where one aspires to perform even better, as well as to situations of underperformance, as illustrated in Table 8.1.

The examples on the left highlight the fact that there is no immediate issue, but there is an aspiration to be in an even better position. It's proactive. The effective problem-solver asks, "How should we get to our aspiration? What's our best strategic choice to get there, given multiple?"

Table 8.1 Typical PSM Applications

Aspirational (Strategy)	Underperformance (Improvement)
"How can we capitalize on this opportunity?"	"How can we recover from the impact of the ignored opportunity?"
"How can company X gain even more market share?"	"Why is company X losing market share, and how can they recover it?"
"How can new operational or commercial capabilities give us a bigger competitive advantage?"	"Why is this operation or process not working well?"

They will define the optimal solution to close that aspirational gap and seize that opportunity. It's about selecting the optimal strategic route to create and sustain a competitive advantage to be superior in an industry. This is strategy.

The examples on the right, the underperformance ones, highlight a problem that is noticeably causing a negative impact and needs to be fixed. It's reactive. The effective problem-solver asks, "Why is this happening and what is the most effective way to fix it?" They will define the optimal solution to close that gap. After properly defining and scoping the problem first, problem solvers conduct a diagnostic phase that identifies the root causes of that gap through analysis, observation, and fact-driven approaches. They prioritize root causes by how much each contributes to the overall gap. They create alternative solutions for each prioritized root cause, assess and prioritize such solutions, and then transform the most attractive solutions into an action plan that will eliminate the gap when executed. This is operational effectiveness.

Companies hire management consultants to solve a problem they can't solve themselves, typically because there is a lack of internal expertise or bandwidth. Different consulting firms have slightly different methodologies here, but the steps are typically relatively similar. According to a McKinsey paper, "The best problem solvers continually develop innovative and impactful insights and solutions; they are comprehensive, fact based, flexible, creative, and pragmatic."[2]

---

[2] I. Davis, D. Keeling, P. Schreier, and A. Williams. July 2007. "The McKinsey Approach to Problem Solving." *McKinsey Staff Paper*, no. 66.

Problem-solving is one of the key skills that I learned and refined during my five years in consulting, through rigorous training and constant practice from one project to the next. Later, I magnified this skill when tasked to train all of Restaurant Brands International's global corporate employees on PSM. Using the skill is one thing, but teaching and coaching others forced me to dive deeper into it and be the face of it. I also trained teams at my current company, and of course continued to apply PSM in my roles—it's my weapon of choice.

The beauty of having this strength is that I can apply it everywhere, even in situations where I lack any expertise on the topic, provided I have access to people who know the topic well but lack knowledge on how to go about effectively solving the problem at hand.

At McKinsey, I used PSM to help a snacks company accelerate sales growth, for instance. But let me tell you about a more challenging project. I was staffed as the project manager to help a European steelmaker in Brazil improve the production capacity of their operation. I felt a bit intimidated as I knew nothing about steelmaking ... absolutely zero! The plant's real output only reached about 70 percent of the designed capacity and they were expecting a surge in demand, a surge they weren't capable of meeting—which would cost them millions in lost sales. Fortunately, a few things were in my favor: Bright people in my team as usual, my knowledge of PSM, and access to metallurgy experts ready to answer any technical questions.

We applied PSM with rigor from week one, and slowly but surely, the root causes started to appear. It took many interviews, a lot of data analysis, conversations with experts in Germany, and replicating the behavior of the plant in a model. PSM enabled us to understand which processing steps were not performing as designed and how we could fix them. We identified the proper solutions for each identified root cause and created a detailed implementation roadmap with over 50 mid-term initiatives to not only meet but exceed designed capacity. The client's internal experts could not solve it on their own. The combination of structured PSM plus content expertise from the internal and external experts created magical results.

I share this personal example of a main spike to also say I built this expertise through years of training, practice in multiple contexts, reading more about it, pondering over it, teaching it, coaching others, and so on. As John C. Maxwell stated, "You never really know something until you teach it to someone else." Teaching enabled me to really go deep. You should consider teaching others, it will force you to become smarter at that topic, and therefore build some serious expertise.

> *The most serious mistakes are not being made as a result of wrong answers. The true dangerous thing is asking the wrong question.*
> —Peter Drucker, Austrian-American management guru and author (1909–2005)

Secondary Spikes

The main spike must be accompanied by other smaller spikes in essential variables for your field—this adds breadth. Otherwise, you become a wild card with clear trade-offs. Some people won't give you the opportunity because you don't check the boxes for other important criteria. "Let's not bring Tom into this, he's super strong in operations but I don't have time to babysit him through all the necessary Excel models we need to build," for example.

You need to minimize those trade-offs to continue growing as a successful professional in your field. If you're a wine salesperson with incredible selling abilities, to get to the next level as an area manager overseeing multiple salespersons, you need sharp team management skills, clear ability to coach your team on finding opportunities to increase sales, and so on. Your key sales strength is excellent, but it needs to be complemented by other skills and abilities. Expect those spikes to change as your grow. For me, those secondary spikes include:

- Leadership skills
- Project management
- Negotiations
- Communications

Of course, the list of topics that are not my secondary spikes is much longer. From a leadership perspective, I have managed and led multiple teams with and without formal authority to accomplish a mission. In my first job out of college, I led a Quality Assurance department and experienced firing, hiring, coaching, and developing my team. During the chocolate project in Brazil, I led over 25 colleagues, where only one of them reported to me directly. Managing teams across the continent sharpened my cultural sensitivity to be more effective. Training has contributed immensely to shaping my leadership skills. You can never stop learning about leadership, it's something you must always build on and continue to sharpen. I've managed so many truly awesome people, plus a handful of difficult or mediocre ones. Every time, there are different leadership tools to apply and lessons to take away. Surely, this is one area we must realize we are WIP.

I formed the other secondary spikes through tons of training and practice throughout the years, sometimes teaching. I have led or co-led dozens of projects, have been trained in Project Management, and therefore trained others. I've done several hundred presentations since business school and have trained hundreds on how to create well-structured presentations. I've taken an interest in negotiations, so I read many books because I realize am always negotiating. Do you have a spouse, boss, kids, or customers? There you go, you too are constantly negotiating, so consider it a valuable secondary spike for you to build—regardless of your field.

The expertise I have built over the years shaped me into who I am professionally. Am I the best leader, the best negotiator, or the best thought partner? Nah, I know people better than me in each of those topics, but I have pretty good performance across those secondary spikes that complement my main spike and make me a well-rounded businessman who can solve critical business problems.

That's all you need: One or two main spikes and a few secondary spikes. Remember though, you must continue sharpening those skills to avoid losing competitive advantage, especially as the topic evolves. This explains why it is tough to have too many spikes. Focus on the ones that matter to achieve your goals in your profession.

Depth and Breadth

Besides the secondary spikes, we should have average performance in a wide range of other relevant topics. Figure 8.1 showed several variables at average performance. Depending on your profession you will need show some level of proficiency in more than 10 topics; the 10 illustrated in Figure 8.1 are just a prioritized list of the top 10.

For instance, I am good at excel—enough to do most of the tasks needed by myself—but not awesome. I would never consider it a secondary spike and I rely on analysts or excel masters to do the more complex models and analysis.

In conclusion, the combination of a main spike or two, a handful of secondary spikes, and sufficient performance on other topics that matter will give you a competitive advantage. Note that this is a general rule and there are exceptions: Some fields require deep specialization. You'd want your brain surgeon to be a rock star at brain surgery, that's it. Finally, per Principle 3, envision Figure 8.1 evolving over time as your spikes evolve and as new topics are added to the mix.

Eric MS and MW

Let me tell you about my colleague Eric, a true world-class example of what deep expertise is, in a fun yet complex topic. As a young man, Eric began working as a waiter's assistant in a highly respected steakhouse in West Palm Beach. At the time, this restaurant had one of the finest wine programs in South Florida. The general manager held a mandatory meeting every Saturday morning at 9 a.m. to increase the wine knowledge plus sales and service skills of the servers, most of whom hated attending such an early meeting.

This is where Eric promptly became fascinated with wine and began to study and taste whenever he got the opportunity. He soon realized that he wanted to build a career in the wine business. When he got promoted to a management position, he got to know a gentleman who later invited him to join the company that is now Southern Glazer's Wine & Spirits (SGWS). His early wine knowledge allowed him to advance at a fast pace in sales and sales management over the next decade.

His next phase at the company was in a newly created wine education position in Florida. After starting, he decided to get an official wine certification to help him in this role. The Society of Wine Educators offered the Certified Wine Educator (CWE) accreditation, and he began studying for it and achieved the credential two years later. About the same time as he began studying for CWE, he signed up for the Court of

Master Sommeliers (CMS) Introductory Course (the one I told you earlier I took). After passing the first CMS level, the content posed an exponentially greater challenge as he prepared for the Advanced Sommelier exam, an extreme leap forward in terms of required theory, service, and blind tasting expertise. It took him two attempts to pass the Advanced exam, during his third year in the role.

But Eric wanted more. He formed a group of like-minded individuals and they began to practice and study toward their common goal of becoming Master Sommeliers. The biggest challenge for Eric became finding time for the intense level of study required while also juggling a full-time job and his family. Fortunately, both were highly supportive, and this encouragement kept him moving forward when he felt like giving up.

He recalls his examination days, which besides the intense theoretical 70 verbal Q&A and demonstrating wine servicing techniques included blind tasting. "I had to taste six wines from anywhere around the world, and correctly identify the region, grape, style, quality level, vintage of at least four to pass." It all paid off, and he became a Master Sommelier (MS) in his sixth year in the role!

But wait, he didn't stop there. Mel, a key executive in the company, told Eric about another program offered by the Institute of Masters of Wine, the Master of Wine (MW) program. This is widely considered the ultimate challenge in the world of wine. The MW program encompasses wine only, unlike MS, but in a much broader scope including viticulture and winemaking, quality assurance, the business of wine (from bulk wines to the world's finest wines), and contemporary wine issues. He passed the MW tasting exam on his first attempt, which meant blind tasting 36 wines over three days and writing appropriate descriptions about each.

Then came the marathon of preparing for the theoretical portion, which he ultimately passed six long years later. To be successful, he deeply learned the science and business underlying the world of wine, and how to write about it both concisely and precisely in timed essay format. "There were many times that I felt I had reached the limits of my endurance and wanted to give up, but the thought of letting Mel, myself and my family down kept me going." The ultimate triumph came eight years after starting the program, upon the successful completion of the dissertation and being awarded the title of MW.

These achievements have rewarded Eric with promotions to Senior Vice President in charge of corporate wine education for the country. This rewarding position has enabled him to expand wine educational programs throughout the vast company network and travel through all wine regions. Eric and his team have overseen more than 10,000 SGWS employee certifications in wine, spirits, and sake programs, creating the best trained sales force in the country.

In life, the MW program has helped Eric develop deep analytical skills and take a 360-degree view of all topics and challenges in life, not just in wine. He picked up French along the way too, just to build his credibility when speaking about French wines. Despite his achievements, Eric acts as if he is a WIP and continues to learn. To stay current in an ever-evolving topic, Eric spends an hour a day reading periodicals and international trade publications.

"There's three words that I would repeat to myself as my mantra over and over as I worked myself through the programs: Patience, perseverance, and determination," he told me as my podcast guest. Eric Hemer went from a waiter's assistant to one of only four people in the world who has ever achieved both MS and MW degrees! His spike in wine knowledge is off the charts. Equally amazing is how down-to-earth, humble, and friendly my coworker down the hall is.

Wrap-Up

Ensure you are building the right expertise to open the doors you want to open. Be strategic about which spikes you will invest time and effort into building, given your field. Your expertise will become a key differentiating factor that builds your professional brand. "A high level of expertise in your field makes you a versatile and valuable employee able to excel in many different facets of your business. It stands you above and apart from others in your field," explains Eric.

The one who gets wisdom loves life; the one who cherishes understanding will soon prosper.

—Proverbs 19:8

Take-Aways: Build Expertise

- You must have superior performance—a main spike—in at least one topic relevant to your profession.
- The main spike(s) must be complemented with secondary spikes in other relevant topics, or else you become a trade-off instead of a desired asset.
- Knowing what those relevant topics are in your world is critical to selecting where you want to build or strengthen spikes—aligned with your strengths, interests, and values.
- It will take time, effort, sweat, and perhaps tears to properly build such expertise and keep it relevant.

Self-Assessment

Which statement describes you best? Circle the corresponding letter.

a. I do not have one or two main spikes of expertise. There are several people in my team or unit that can do exactly what I do. I'm a jack of all trades and master of none.

b. I am making progress building and sharpening my one or two main spikes and have more work to do. I have a few secondary spikes ... and a few areas to address.

c. I possess one or two well-developed main spikes, complemented by three to six secondary spikes. To excel in my role, I have addressed weaknesses in areas that matter in my field.

Actions

- Think about your profession and write down a list of up to 10 key skills (hard and soft) that an effective leader must have.

Variables: Score:

A. _____   _____

B. _____   _____

C. _____   _____

D. _____   _____

E. _____   _____

F. _____   _____

G. _____   _____

H. _____   _____

I. _____   _____

J. _____   _____

- Knowing what you know about yourself (passions, strengths, and turn-offs), place an asterisk next to any skills on the list that you believe can help differentiate you, if they were your one or two main spikes and two to five secondary spikes.
- Now that you have defined that list, go back and score yourself 1 to 10 points, relative to others in your field (peers and leaders).
- Plot each score in the chart and connect the dots with a line. These are variables in the x-axis in Figure 8.2.
- What is the chart telling you?
  - If you have spikes in the skills with asterisks: That is awesome! Keep investing time and effort to maintain those spikes.
  - If you have gaps between your score and where a main or secondary spike would be, create a brief action plan for each

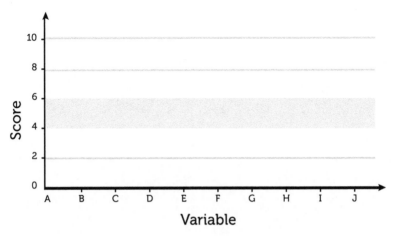

Figure 8.2 Plot of Key Skills in Your Field—To Complete

one, specifying what actions you can take to start building that expertise (mentors to talk to, projects to engage with, training to attend, books to read ...). Set deadlines and place calendar reminders. Commit!

Gap to close: _____   <u>Target date:</u>
Actions: _____   _____
                _____   _____
                _____   _____
                _____   _____

Gap to close: _____
Actions: _____   _____
                _____   _____
                _____   _____
                _____   _____

Gap to close: _____
Actions: _____   _____
                _____   _____
                _____   _____
                _____   _____

- Track your expertise-building journey. Periodically assess your performance versus your field's essential variables in case new ones arise or more work is needed in the current variables.

CHAPTER 9

Define Your Brand

A brand for a company is like a reputation for a person. You earn reputation by trying to do hard things well.

—Jeff Bezos, American self-made billionaire

Why Should You?

Now it's time to bring your strengths, values, and main spike(s) into a cohesive story: Your brand. Look around you: The clothes you are wearing, your shoes, your accessories, and your gadgets. As I look around me, I see my *Garmin* GPS watch that I use for running, my *Bose* noise cancelling Bluetooth headphones, the ubiquitous *Apple* iPhone, *Trident* gum, and other brands. Chances are you have a degree of loyalty to the key brands in your life. That is because you have grown to trust them more than the alternatives. They represent a good level of quality, dependability, comfort, and whatever other attribute you value in that product, for the price you paid. You are probably a repeat customer for certain brands, because if you are satisfied with a brand's performance, it simplifies the replacement process. True, some people are not too brand loyal, and for some products, brands can be irrelevant, but that does not reduce the importance of brands in general.

Like any product or company, you also have a brand whether you know it or not. The sooner you are in control of defining what that brand is and what is associated with it, the better. If you don't define it, other people will define it for you, and you might not like the outcome.

A brand helps differentiate you from those around you (colleagues, classmates, or competition). It helps communicate a message that conveys to people what they can expect from you, what your competencies are, and what you bring to the table. It also gives you focus and purpose. For professional matters, this is critical since it helps create a reputation that creates (or destroys) demand for your services and involvement. Not just because of what you can accomplish, but how you go about it as a leader, manager, peer, or follower.

Your brand is what makes people want to work with you, what makes hiring managers want to hire you, and what makes senior leaders want to give you increased responsibilities. A well-established and strong brand leads to: "She is the guru in this topic, and she's awesome to work with. We need her!" In contrast, a horrible brand makes others say "Ugh, avoid him at all costs, he sucks!" Like a savvy marketer building consumer brands through carefully designed strategies and tactics aimed at influencing consumers' perception, you must have conscious control of your brand and how other people perceive it.

Author Robert Greene includes our reputation—or brand—as one of his 48 laws of power, and states, "Your reputation inevitably precedes you, and if it inspires respect, a lot of your work is done for you before you arrive on the scene, or utter a single word."[1]

Professional Brand Statement

Your personal brand should be one sentence long. It should express your core strengths, skills, and even values in a way that makes people think of you when they think of that topic. Of course, defining yourself in one sentence is tough, it's a general description of you: There is only so much you can mention. Select well. A good example is: "Mariana is a trustworthy financial planner in San Diego helping young couples start their investment journey to maximize long-term wealth creation." Or: "Paola is a top-rated, easy-to-work-with, real estate agent of choice for foreigners buying and selling high-end properties in Palm Beach." Note the brands convey focus. Don't call Mariana if you need tax return help or if you are retiring soon because there are better choices for that. Mariana should also not market her services to people about to retire—her actions should reinforce that focus. Similarly, don't call Paola if you need a starter home in Miami. That's the power of the brand, it helps people think of you for a specific need where you outshine the competition.

---

[1] R. Greene. 2000. *The 48 Laws of Power.* Penguin Books.

This dynamic is the same as for products: If a friend asks me for a recommendation for a lovely Champagne for their at-home anniversary dinner, I can confidently recommend specific brands depending on how much they are willing to spend. I trust the brands I would recommend will deliver the experience that my friend is looking for. I associated a need (impressive dinner) with a solution (a Champagne brand I trust and enjoy) and I matched my friend and the product ... that is what you want others to do when they think of the topic you master.

Phil, the Agent of Change

I've known many colleagues who succeeded at building a solid professional brand. For example, when I think of change management, I immediately think of my Canadian ex-colleague Phil, who I met while at Cadbury.

Let's briefly define change management to better understand what Phil does. It is the structured approach to manage the people side of a change initiative as they adopt new ways of thinking and behaving to achieve the desired outcomes. Many of the business problems I've stepped in to fix, stemmed from poor change management when the organization introduced a change—proper change management is a must to make new attitudes and behaviors stick.

During the pandemic, why do you think the United States struggled to get its population to consistently implement the medical recommendation to wear masks that helps filter the air we breathe, to limit the spread of an airborne respiratory virus? Because we lacked a well-designed, consistent change management program at the federal, state, and county level that was consistently executed to change the attitudes and behavior of different subgroups in society (the message tailored to address each subgroups' interests and concerns). There was no unified and consistent communication and training plan to educate people and convince them the requested behavior has greater benefits than downsides. As we can now all appreciate, the effects of failed change management can be evident.

Phil obtained his bachelor's in Commerce, with elective classes in Organizational Behavior and People, from the University of Toronto.

When we met, he was the Vice President of Organizational Change. We intersected in several projects and training events. His brand statement is: "A global change management expert who helps leaders and their teams achieve their personal and business goals by providing change expertise and skill building." Let's dissect and peel his brand statement into the three elements of strengths, values, and expertise.

Phil is acutely aware he enjoys providing advice and building skills in leadership teams, through teaching, training, coaching, and mentoring—and seeing them succeed at the transformation they embarked on. His strengths and motivators are well aligned with his expertise. He also continued to invest in his learning: Ten years after obtaining his Bachelor of Commerce degree, he went back to the university to obtain a Diploma in Adult Education to sharpen his abilities at coaching business leaders.

From a values perspective, two of his core values are service and empathy. They are embedded or implied in his brand statement through the word "help" and by including his client's *personal goals,* not just business goals. His work often expands to include giving individuals private support, enabling them to be their best during a phase of significant organizational change. These values also led him to work pro bono with not-for-profit organizations.

Phil built his strong professional brand throughout his career by dedicating time and effort to build his expertise—his spikes—after 30 years of leading and managing change across 60 countries and leading over 30 large change initiatives in multiple industries.

One of his biggest initiatives involved co-leading the multiyear postmerger integration of Kraft and Cadbury in 60 countries, where he oversaw the harmonization and creation of policies, back-office and customer-facing processes, and even culture. He explains "I built deep expertise by accumulating experiences, testing ideas, making mistakes, asking leaders for advice, achieving big wins, and doing it in many organizations and industries." Something noteworthy: He built expertise by saying yes to a challenging invitation, as we explored in Chapter 4: He was asked to lead HR for Canada, and despite the fact he lacked HR management experience, he went for it!

It's one thing to define your brand, it's another to activate it. Brand activation is the process by which a marketer executes activities aimed at generating and increasing brand awareness, so consumers have it top of mind. Phil does this brilliantly. He has written over 300 blog posts, launched a podcast focused on change management, speaks at universities, and wrote two award-winning books: *Change with Confidence* and *Change on the Run*. Brand activation is not a one-time effort, it is ongoing.

Phil's brand has also evolved over time. When asked about his brand many years ago when he started his journey, he explains "Oh, even though my work was similar, I was much more insular. I focused on my immediate team and not on holistic organizational efforts. I was also more concerned about my own performance and less about serving others. I did not have some skills back then that I have developed and fine-tuned over the years." Yes, even Phil Buckley's solid professional brand evolves. Your challenge is to manage the evolution according to the strategy you have laid out for your career.

In summary, when I think of change management, or someone asks me if I know an expert in such topic, I think of Phil Buckley. That's what you need to create, the wide-spread association of your name to what you offer as a professional.

Note: Phil may or may not be the best change management guru in the Western Hemisphere. But I believe he is the best one in my network, which is all *he* needs. With my belief, he knows I will recommend him when someone I know is searching for such services. The same applies to you; You don't need to be the best in the world, just one of the best in the world of your contacts. The problem is, sometimes we are one of the best—or the best—in someone's network, but we are not top of mind because we do a poor job of marketing our brand. Don't let this happen to you!

What's Mine?

One more example. Alejandro is *an effective leader and thought partner that solves complex strategic problems to deliver tangible value in the food and beverage industry.* That is my current brand statement as an employee in strategy. So, if a high-tech company needs help solving complex problems, I don't think I'm the guy. If someone needs help with automation technologies in a motorcycle manufacturing plant, or designing a new advertising campaign, they'll get better results with people I can connect them with. But if a food and beverage company—or consumer goods—needs help creating a business strategy to gain market share or increase margin, improving a cross-functional process, identifying the root causes of underperformance, transforming itself, or deciding between strategic choices, I'd be a good match.

Regarding personal traits, note I am not explicitly stating them, but I am implicitly incorporating some:

- Strengths: Analytical, learner, and responsible
- Motivators: Impact, learning, challenge, problem-solving, and excelling
- Values: Hard work/diligence, knowledge, intellectualism, and empathy

Phil did the same with his values of service and empathy. You don't need to artificially insert lots of adjectives, you will know it is coherent when your proposition is logically connected to your strengths, motivators, and values. Just like Phil can't be a strong coach to executives leading transformation if he wasn't empathetic and service oriented, I can't be a good problem solver without a genuine desire to learn new things, be challenged, be analytical, and deliver impact.

The reason why being an effective leader and thought partner are elements in my brand statement is because I believe being highly skilled at something like problem-solving is not enough to differentiate myself in my world. If I were awesome at it, but also an arrogant jerk incapable of managing and leading teams, or unable to provide other strategic services, I would not be the partner of choice. You must be well-rounded in hard and soft skills to be competent and likeable. Loveable Stars are "desperately wanted" high-performers, and Competent Jerks are "mostly avoided" despite their results, according to a Harvard Business Review article.[2] It's not just about your main spike and what you bring to the

---

[2] T. Casciaro, and M. Sousa Lobo. June 2005. "Competent Jerks, Lovable Fools, and the Formation of Social Networks." *Harvard Business Review.*

table, but how well you complement such spike and what type of leader or follower you are. Let's aim to be competent and likeable.

Managing Evolution

Personal brands can and should evolve over time. As you mature you go deeper into a field of expertise or expand the breadth of your expertise, and you sharpen key traits. Sometimes you even reinvent yourself, as when you change career.

If I now create a brand for younger Alejandro before business school, it would be something like: *A highly dedicated, fast-learning, results-driven professional focused on managing and improving food quality systems.* Since then, business school helped expand my skill set from technical to business, multiple roles changed my focus, managing teams across the continent refined my leadership effectiveness, and so on. Although young Alejandro's qualifiers still apply, I choose to emphasize other strengths such as the ability to lead teams and my ability to deliver financial benefits to the companies I work for.

And in a few years, my brand will evolve further—that is perfectly fine. You need to be strategic about that evolution. We will focus next on how to define your current brand, but it is not far-fetched to then design the next version of your brand. This will help you determine the actions needed between now and then to create that diversification, depth, or change your future brand requires of you. First things first, though ...

What's Yours?

After reviewing Phil's brand and mine to get the hang of it, let's focus on yours. To come up with your brand, you need to know yourself well. Determine which strengths, values, and skills, you are better off showcasing —this depends on your overall goal and who is your brand marketing audience. For example, if I wanted a new role in postmerger integration, I would mention that instead of strategy or problem-solving. I have that experience, but it is not exactly how I want to position myself going forward. So, what did you select?

Main spike(s) (strengths):   Values: Expertise:

_____   _____   _____

_____   _____   _____

_____   _____   _____

Next, validate your thoughts by talking to people that know you well who can offer direct and unbiased feedback (your direct reports or your mom may not be the best choices). Based on what you learn, refine your key descriptors. Now create your brand statement, feel free to validate once more: You need to ensure it accurately reflects who you are *today*.

My current brand statement is:

_____

_____

So, what do you do with your brand statement? Use it as a reminder to help take the right course of action (what projects and opportunities to seek to further refine your skills, what training to enroll in, and so forth) and bring it up in conversations to start marketing your professional identity. Your brand is not who you aspire to be, it is who you are *now*: You must back it up this week and next week, or dissatisfied customers will not be recommending your brand anytime soon. It is not aspirational or futuristic.

However, start thinking now how you want your brand to evolve, and by when.

In _____ years, my brand statement should be:

_____

_____

One key element that should influence that evolution is understanding what traits are valued in your current organization or field, or any organization you aspire to join. Once you can name the key attributes to be an even more impactful professional in your current or future organization, assess the gap compared to your current brand attributes. If there is a gap, translate it into an action plan, and seek opportunities to learn and master those desired skills through learning, coaching, practice, and even teaching. This is how your brand helps you identify what investments to make in yourself. When you reach a new level of mastery, you will be able to refresh your brand accordingly.

And finally, remember you must live up to your brand. What you do, what you say, what you don't do, and what you don't say, can build or erode your brand. For instance, imagine a leader in your organization losing control and insulting a colleague in public, causing a scene. There is potential damage to his brand, and the lost respect is difficult and slow to regain, if recoverable. "It takes 20 years to build a reputation and five minutes to ruin it. If you think about that, you'll do things differently," says Warren Buffett.

Wrap-Up

You need to build the association of your name with a topic you master the same way I associate Phil to change management. Define your brand, live up to it, reinforce it, and always invest in increasing your brand equity. Your key traits, values, and expertise help shape your brand. It takes time to build a valuable brand. Take care of it and think strategically about how it should evolve. Like a skillful marketer, create appropriate brand activation initiatives to keep your brand top of mind.

All of us need to understand the importance of branding. We are CEOs of our own companies: Me Inc. To be in business today, our most important job is to be head marketer for the brand called You.
— Tom Peters, American business guru and writer

Take-Aways: Define Your Brand

- You must define your brand before others do it for you.
- Your brand is composed directly by your strengths and expertise, and directly or indirectly by your values.
- Your brand helps convey what you bring to the table, helps differentiate you, and serves as a reminder for what investments to make and what paths to take.
- Your brand will likely evolve. Don't let it just wander off, plan that evolution well.

Self-Assessment

Which statement describes you best? Circle the corresponding letter.

a. I have not designed and created a professional brand to differentiate myself. There are many with my skill set in my organization.

b. I have a good idea what my professional brand is, but I need to be more strategic in designing it, communicating it, and planning its evolution.

c. I possess a clear professional brand that I use to communicate how I add value. I am envisioning how it will evolve over the next 3–5 years, and I am taking steps toward it.

Actions

- If you skipped the exercises above listing your current and future brand … nice try.
- Write down the keywords you believe are more appropriate to describe what you bring to the table based on your **strengths**:

——————————, ——————————, ——————————,

——————————, ——————————, ——————————.

- Now circle the most impactful and relevant ones given your context.
- Write down the keywords you believe are more appropriate to describe what you bring to the table based on your **values**:

  ———————————, ———————————, ———————————,

  ———————————, ———————————, ———————————.

- Now circle the most impactful and relevant ones given your context.
- Write down the keywords you believe are more appropriate to describe what you bring to the table based on your **expertise**:

  ———————————, ———————————, ———————————.

  ———————————, ———————————, ———————————.

- Now circle the most impactful and relevant ones given your context.
- Get feedback from several people that know you well. Ask them what they believe helps you stand out. Validate the circled words.
- With clarity on strengths, values, and expertise, craft a version of your brand statement. You might need to review with people you trust until it accurately describes you.

  _____

  _____.

- Think about how you want your brand to evolve, and by when. In _____ years, my brand statement should be:

  _____

  _____.

- Continue to invest in your brand's key attributes in a manner consistent with its planned evolution.
- Over time, revisit and refine your brand to better capture new versions of an improved You.

End of Part II

Now we have explored how to have the right mindset for your journey
and how to build an attractive brand that differentiates you in your field.

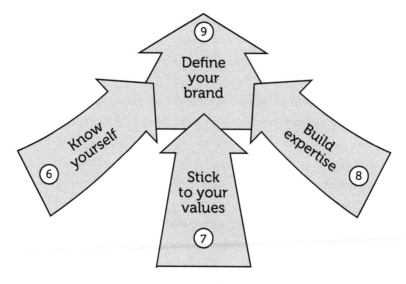

We will now explore how to be more effective in progressing in
your career.

PART III

Be the Driver

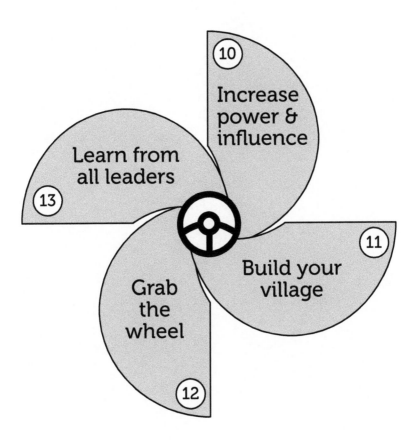

CHAPTER 10

Increase Power and Influence

Before I served as a consultant to Kennedy, I had believed, like most academics, that the process of decision-making was largely intellectual and all one had to do was walk into the president's office and convince him of the correctness of one's view. This perspective I soon realized is as dangerously immature as it is widely held.

—Henry Kissinger, U.S. Secretary of State (1923–1974)

Why Should You?

Some people think all they need to do is put their heads down and deliver great results for success to come. Power and influence are touchy subjects for many because they are easily misinterpreted, misused, and abused—therefore, many avoid it. In some cultures, including in Latin America based on my experience, it is mostly unspoken and untaught—some even associate the quest for power with dirty politicians (which we can all agree to hate). Prof. Alison Fragale, an Organizational Psychologist and Professor of power and influence at University of North Carolina Kenan-Flagler Business School, explained in my podcast why most people unfortunately avoid this topic with these two statements:

- Culturally, we don't like to talk about it. A quote from Rosabeth Moss Kanter, a Harvard Business School professor, captures it well; "Power is America's last dirty word. It's easier to talk about money—and easier to talk about sex—than it is to talk about power."
- The American Dream narrative states "If you work hard you can succeed" which is misinterpreted as a myth of individualism: "If I simply do good work, that will be rewarded. If I

have to do anything else, that's suggesting I did not get here by my own merit," people think.

Because the decision to hire you, or to bring you into that cool project, or give you that international assignment, or to promote you, or to implement your idea, or give you that well-deserved raise is made by others, you must be well-versed in the dynamics of power and influence to grow in your field. This topic is a key principle for career growth even if it's taboo. It can derail or boost you. This is something I didn't fully grasp until I started studying it in business school, and I will share my learnings with you.

Like me, you are part of an organization: A team, a company, a university, or a government institution. Like it or not, we must realize that organizations are political entities, and that power, influence, and politics are used to achieve the organization's goals and individual's goals. The goals we pursue can be positive or negative, but power is neutral.

Let's start with two key definitions:

1. Power is the ability to change people's behavior. That ability comes from something you possess at that moment in time.
2. Influence is the set of actions through which people use their power to change behavior or attitudes.

In other words, power is a noun—something you own which you don't use all the time. Influence is a verb—an action taken. The more power you have, the more influential you can be. Power and influence help you get things done in your organization; thus, they are your friends. You need to learn how to influence others because success depends on how well you work with and through others. If I possess the best idea and the right solution to solve a critical business problem, but if I can't influence others to support and implement it, I generate no value for my organization. This was especially true for me as a Director of Americas Operations Development at Cadbury. I had to work through multiple country teams scattered across the continent from Toronto to Buenos Aires—none reporting to me—to drive the expected results my corporate team envisioned.

The benefits of being perceived as influential and savvy in power dynamics within your organization or field are that you:

- Are less likely to face opposition; thus, you can get things done more efficiently
- Build a reputation of being someone reliable who gets the job done
- Are given more stimulating challenges and opportunities
- Become better equipped to bring and lead change
- Have an easier time getting allies and followers
- Get access to mentors with more power
- Get more training opportunities
- Enjoy higher job satisfaction

Who doesn't want these benefits? In essence, power and influence build your reputation as a high performer because they help you deliver results. When you make your boss and your team look good, you look good.

To succeed in an organization, Jeffrey Pfeffer, Professor of Organizational Behavior at the Graduate School of Business at Stanford University, proposes in *Managing With Power* that you need intelligence, expertise, drive, *and* a good match between your political skills and the political skills that your position requires.[1] Depending on your role, you can get away with having low power, but as you grow into a higher position of leadership, this becomes a key skill you can't do without. For example, a Chief Information Officer needs much more influence and power to be effective than one of her junior programmers, whose performance heavily—but not exclusively—relies on technical skills. This analogy also illustrates another concept confirmed by Prof. Fragale: The higher you go up the hierarchy, the more relevant power and influence become. Therefore, not only do you need it now, you'll need to get more proficient at it as you grow.

---

[1] J. Pfeffer. 1992. *Managing with Power.* Harvard Business School Press.

Now that we've clarified the importance of power and influence in achieving a specific goal within your organization, and more importantly in your career, let's explore how you can identify sources of power within your organization and grow your power. Let me say it again though: Power is not negative—provided your goals are constructive and positive. You *need* more power and influence.

Understand the Landscape

Within your organization, power is not distributed equally. Some teams, departments, business units, or individuals have more power than others. Your first task is to understand the lay of the land: Identify the relative power of the people and teams around you and understand their interests. Pragmatically, you can talk to people and ask the right questions and observe. There are fancier techniques but let's keep it simple.

You will hear stories such as "Wow, the supply chain head got ripped apart in the executive meeting, even though the issue seems to have been caused by the commercial team. The CEO treats him like a second-class citizen!" This is something I said many years ago after witnessing it live in an organization where the CEO didn't value the supply chain team's contributions. Or you'll hear, "Mark just got a new team added to his scope, and some of the top talent from that division joined him." Or it goes like this, "Our budget just got slashed, but they increased Walter's budget significantly." See the pattern? These are obvious examples of relative power differences or shifts. Some are not obvious and require more digging and careful observation.

You can assess relative power in your organization by gaining insights about:

- Reputational indicators: Asking around and making conclusions based on teams' and individuals' reputations. Who has the attention and trust of your organization's leader?
- Representational indicators: Knowing which teams or functions are over-represented in key committees and who is present when key decisions are made.

- Decision outcomes: Observing who benefits from corporate decisions when funds are reallocated, promotions are given, initiatives are approved, teams are restructured, and so on.
- Symbols of power: Observing who has the best physical space (nicer views or larger offices) or the best perks. That said, some organizations are better than others at minimizing physical space differentiation and office space is becoming less relevant with higher acceptance of work-from-home arrangements.

Once you know more about how power is distributed in your organization, the next step is to understand the interests of the different parties, especially on matters that concern you and your responsibilities. Who is likely to block your interests? Why? Who is likely to support your interests? Why? Without this knowledge, you will have a harder time negotiating to get your ideas implemented.

Now you need to strategize how to get powerful teams or individuals to support you and how to neutralize blockers. This is not a Machiavellian activity: It is common sense applied to making your voice heard and ensuring that your recommendations are implemented. You need to think about how to make them understand that your idea (about a business topic or your career progression) supports or doesn't contradict their interests, or you need to tell the story differently to draw those parallels out rather than just relying on hard facts.

Identify the Right Places

The upside of doing your homework is you will learn who has more power, but the downside is you may learn you are not in a high-power team. According to *Power, Influence, and Persuasion*, working for a manager with clout "confers an aura of status" and brings "visibility, upward mobility, and resources" but "powerlessness tends to breed bossiness rather than true leadership," and "working for a powerless boss is like being in the outer darkness."[2] Which manager would you rather work for?

---

[2] 2005. *Power, Influence, and Persuasion*. Harvard Business School Press.

Teams with more power:

- Are closer to the organization's high-priority initiatives
- Are closer to key information or are "in the know"
- Have bigger budgets, which is critical in many ways
- Easily attract and retain top talent and have faster promotion tracks
- Have more access to training
- Might have bigger and better office space and perks
- Have higher compensation and faster growth for its members

As a matter of fact, a study of 338 managers proved this last point: Employees beginning their careers in higher power departments showed more rapid movement through the organization, and the power of one's initial department plays a continuing role in salary in career progression.[3] In several companies, I learned about compensation gaps for people with the same title and seniority but in different functions. Of course, your HR department will not e-mail you a compensation spreadsheet upon request, but eventually you can piece insights together. Key lesson: It's important to be in the right team if you want access to more budget, better training, faster promotions, higher compensation, higher impact work, more exposure, and so on.

After you understand which groups have more power, don't stop there. That is just a snapshot of the current state. Now try to understand how power might be shifting. Will those that have the power edge today have it in two years? Five years? Tough to know with certainty, but if you are savvy enough you can identify trends and patterns and visualize where power is moving toward. This could be useful information for planning internal career moves. You might have to decide between Team X that has more power now, or Team Z that has less but making the right moves to grow its power base.

---

[3] J.E. Sheridan, J.W. Slocum, Jr., R. Buda, and R.C. Thompson. 2017. "Effects of Corporate Sponsorship and Departmental Power on Career Tournaments." *Academy of Management* 33, no. 3, pp. 578–602.

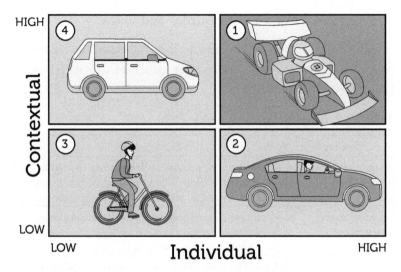

Figure 10.1 The Road to Champagne© power matrix

As Figure 10.1 illustrates, there are two types of power sources, visualized as a matrix. You must work your way to the right by increasing your individual power sources, and upward by increasing your contextual power sources. *Individual* power sources depend on you and your traits and capabilities. *Contextual* power sources depend on your position within your organization (or industry if you are already making a splash beyond your organization).

There are ways to move closer into Race Car territory (Zone #1)—and therefore get to Champagne faster. We all are in different spots now, and what is important is being knowledgeable about this key topic to think strategically about how to increase your power sources. Yes, I've been in all four quadrants. No, don't panic if you're not where you need to be.

Note I depict the car in Zone #2 to be faster than the one in Zone #3: If you have are in Zone #4 and you move to a team with lower power, you enter Bicycle territory because you have not yet developed your individual power sources well. That is why I would prefer being in Zone #2 rather than #4. It means you built solid individual power sources, and a move to the right team boosts you to Zone #1!

Your Power Sources and Gaps

Based on my experience and research, the main individual and contextual potential sources of power you can leverage are summarized in the following tables (Tables 10.1 and 10.2).

Table 10.1 **Individual power sources**

Source	Description
Awareness of the dynamic	Knowledge is power, especially regarding your understanding of the organization's power dynamic. If you don't understand it, you can't effectively navigate it.
Reputation and track record	Meeting and exceeding expectations increases your credibility and power. This is a key source for you, and guess what? You fully control it.
Focused expertise	A study revealed *"The particular expertise acquired by concentrating on a narrow range of business issues is helpful in building a power base and in becoming successful."*[4] This reinforces the need for expertise covered in Chapter 8.
Emotional intelligence	Ironically, understanding the interests and positions of others not only helps you relate to them, but also helps you achieve your own interests. Double whammy!
Marketability	If you are a high performer with options, you increase negotiating power when it comes to your career path.
Likeability	Being perceived as charismatic, engaging, admired, well-spoken, and knowledgeable increases your power. Physical attractiveness also plays a role—we can't do much about our genes, but there are many aspects we control like our choice of clothes, hairstyle, neatness, and so on
Relationships	According to *Power, Influence, and Persuasion*, having relationships with influential people or being part of coalitions affect your power.[5] This is critical and I'll devote the next chapter to it!
Tolerating conflict	If you shy away from conflict, you'll have a tougher time getting what you want. You must be willing to engage in healthy conflict to defend the right position. Bold ideas generate resistance.
Sharp influencing skills	Being skilled at applying multiple influence and negotiation strategies and tactics enhances your power.

---

[4] 2005. *Power, Influence, and Persuasion*. Harvard Business School Press.

[5] J.E. Sheridan, J.W. Slocum, Jr., R. Buda, and R.C. Thompson. 2017. "Effects of Corporate Sponsorship and Departmental Power on Career Tournaments." *Academy of Management* 33, no. 3, pp. 578–602

Table 10.2 Contextual power sources

Source	Description
Being in the right team	Being in a more powerful team within your organization increases your power. Others associate you with the power of the team you belong to.
Communication network position	The more your team is plugged into the organization's communication flow, the higher access to key information—this increases power.
Authority	A bigger title gives you more power, especially if in the right team. That promotion matters. Also, last names matter if they associate you with powerful individuals. But don't depend on this power source, it can impact morale around you and even backfire.
Resources	Managing key resources such as people, knowledge, and funds that others need increases your power. People don't want to be on your blacklist for fear of less access to those required resources.

Now, let's do a power assessment. Give yourself an objective score of 1 to 10 in each power source (5 being average proficiency). Be honest with yourself and potentially ask for feedback from trusted colleagues. With solid self-awareness (as explained in Chapter 6), you can paint an accurate picture of your power sources. Skip the Gap column for now, you'll come back to it.

- Individual   Score: Gap:
  - Awareness of the dynamic   _____   _____
  - Reputation and track record   _____   _____
  - Focused expertise   _____   _____
  - Emotional intelligence   _____   _____
  - Marketability   _____   _____
  - Likeability   _____   _____
  - Relationships   _____   _____
  - Tolerating conflict   _____   _____
  - Sharp influencing skills   _____   _____
- Contextual
  - Being in the right team   _____   _____
  - Communication network position   _____   _____

　　o Authority   _____   _____
　　o Resources   _____   _____

Are you currently strong in several of these power sources? Are there some you need to improve? It is tough to master them all. Think strategically about which sources you are better positioned to strengthen and use going forward—this depends on your current organization and role and the power requirements of your next desired move. However, aspire and work to be adequately proficient in most.

- For each power source, determine how large the gap is to reach a performance target of 7.5 (i.e., the midpoint between the center of the scale and the right extreme) by subtracting your self-score from 7.5 (leave the gap as zero if you scored above 7.5): write it down in the last column above.
  - o 7.5 is my generalized target, though you can go a little lower or higher depending on the power needs of your position.
  - o If you are already close to the target, that's awesome! Sure, you can improve, but I would focus that energy elsewhere as explained next.
- Circle your biggest three gaps.
- Fine-tune your prioritization by rearranging the order based on what power sources are valued or esteemed more in your organization. For example, if you have two gaps of similar size for Relationships and Tolerating Conflict—and in your organization "who you know" is critical to success—focus first on improving your Relationships power source.
- Summarize here what sources you prioritized:
  - o Priority 1: _____
  - o Priority 2: _____
  - o Priority 3: _____

How to Move Right

As illustrated in Figure 10.2, moving right on the matrix, or increasing your individual power sources, is achievable.

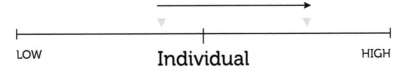

LOW   **Individual**   HIGH

Figure 10.2 Axis of Individual Power

There is no secret, it just requires strategic thinking, conscious planning, and action. In the following tables (Tables 10.3 and 10.4), let's explore

Table 10.3 Increasing individual power

Source	Actions
Awareness of the dynamic	Start paying closer attention to how your organization works based on the "Understanding the Landscape" section. Learn more through courses or books (I've done both and will keep reading more about this topic).
Reputation and track record	You need to consistently shine and excel in your current role. Sorry, there are no short-cuts. Your brand must involve excellence and consistent delivery.
Focused expertise	Dedicate time and effort to build and maintain main and secondary spikes, as discussed in Chapter 8.
Emotional intelligence	Training and studying are key. Keep improving—always be WIP (work in progress) in this area, as explored in Chapter 6 and 13.
Marketability	Create a brand, as in Chapter 9, that is transferable to other teams or organizations. The higher the demand for your services, the greater your options are and this augments your power.
Likeability	Understand which traits are highly valued in your organization and apply them. Some are obvious (i.e., be respectful, greet others, and dress well) and others require more effort (i.e., proficient public speaking, building rapport, and having executive presence).
Relationships	Establish good relationships with the people you identified as well-plugged into your organization's power. Get allies to support your ideas. More in Chapter 11.
Tolerating conflict	Learn to separate *issue* conflict from *personal* conflict—conflict doesn't have to sour relationships. Depending on what you are trying to achieve, expect different levels of conflict. Explore books or courses on increasing conflict tolerance.
Sharp influencing skills	Like any other skill, invest the time to become proficient. Training, books, and coaching will help you apply multiple strategies and tactics. For example, I took a two-day "Strategies for Enhancing Executive Influence" course to learn more, years after taking a class in business school.

Table 10.4 Increasing contextual power

Source	Action
Being in the right team	As described earlier, identify, target, and work toward joining them. A more strenuous route is working to increase the power of your team: This entails changing its scope, priorities, and positioning.
Communication network position	Get closer to in-the-know people. Have lunch with them, help them out, and form authentic mutually beneficial relationships.
Authority	Yes, continue climbing the organization's ladder for bigger roles and titles. However, do not rely on this source. Tossing your title around gets old and frustrates people. Convince them: Don't coerce them even if you can.
Resources	When possible, prefer roles that manage something of value to others (i.e., information, people in demand, budgets, or access). Increase the scope of your current role.

a few concise yet tangible steps you can take to increase your power in each source, keeping focus on your newly discovered priorities.

After my business school summer internship at Kearney and before joining them full time as an Associate, I assessed my power sources relative to a similar list to think strategically about my approach to succeeding there. Reputation is a huge power source to have in management consulting firms: It influences evaluations, progression, and project staffing decisions. So, I created a high-level action plan for the Reputation and Track Record source, including defining the reputation I sought to create. I would establish my reputation as someone recognized for:

- Having initiative and performing in any challenge
- Being creative and cooperative
- Being liked and admired by clients
- Being interested in the well-being and development of the firm

After building a good reputation, I became better armed for conversations with partners about my interest to participate in their upcoming project, and therefore had more control over my career (who to work with, what industry or topic to be exposed to, what expertise to start building, and so on). All my super bright colleagues and I needed to get things done for the client, the firm, and ourselves; therefore, we had to work hard at increasing our power to be more effective, starting with Reputation and Track Record. Know where to focus given your organization's dynamics.

How to Move Upwards

Now let's explore how to move upward along the contextual axis, as shown in the Figure 10.3.

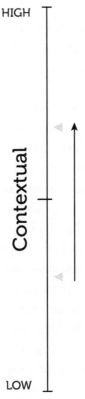

Figure 10.3 Axis of contextual power

To move upward, you might need to change where you are within the organization (or change organizations, but let's stick with the former). Once you know where power is, start exercising your influence skills and get closer to it. Get to know the leaders and peers there, get involved in their projects and initiatives, and identify a role where you can be plugged into the communication flow. This will expose you to hot topics that matter and will connect you with influential people who can have positive impact on your career.

> If you are still a bit skeptic about the importance of power and influence, let me remind you the alternative is watching others tackle the hot topics that matter, and not having the right exposure and mentorship.

An important premise is that you and I have transferable skills. If you are an IT specialist (let's assume with specific skills only relevant in an IT department), chances are you will remain in the IT department of your organization regardless of its power base. However, your next move can be to a highly visible IT project or team within IT, or even to a company where IT holds the greatest power relative to other functions. Even in these scenarios, it would confirm you have transferrable skills to go beyond your current scope.

Let's explore brief concrete steps you can take to increase your power in each source.

Sometimes, you get plucked into the right team—rarely by luck, though! When I worked at Sea Farms Group, I was among a handful of functional leaders chosen to help design and set up a new cooking plant to export frozen ready-to-eat shrimp. I then led the QA department once operational. This new project became the center of attention of investors, customers, and leadership. I didn't realize it clearly then, but that became the company's new power center of gravity.

I wrote this about 20 years ago in a paper for my Power and Politics class at Kellogg:

> I was fortunate to land in the most powerful unit within the company, having a perfect position for networking and exposing

my abilities to important constituencies, and being able to prove to others I am capable of any challenge, thus helping the company succeed. I guess at that time I wasn't trying to be strategic, but I'm glad I used those opportunities the way I did, or I wouldn't be here.

Indeed, succeeding in the power unit gave me the right achievements and references to be admitted at Kellogg.

More often than not, you must *actively* move into the right team. Several times in my career, I realized that my team did not place in the VIP section of the organization' power rankings. What caught my attention about the more powerful teams included the buzz about them, their scope of work, their exciting achievements, and the growth trajectory of their members—the consequences of having power, not the power itself. These were typically the revenue-generating teams that drove initiatives shaping the company's success, and most company executives grew out of those teams.

I asked myself "How can I create a win-win scenario, where the team benefits from my membership and I benefit from belonging to the team?" Again, notice there is nothing Machiavellian about leveraging the power dynamic to move forward with a proposal where both parties will truly benefit at the expense of no one.

The answer has been relatively similar in all scenarios. I made my current manager aware of my future interests during career path conversations to obtain their support and avoid any roadblocks. I met the executive leading a fascinating team to express my interest in joining their team and to explain how I would add value. I elaborated on my brand proposition and how I can help them solve the key strategic issues they were facing. I leveraged several of my power sources: Reputation and track record, focused expertise, marketability, and likeability. These leaders either knew me and saw my work and character firsthand or validated my capabilities through future work triggered by that initial interaction. Because I delivered on my promise to achieve high-quality results, they all later invited me to join them.

Note that I joined them not because I felt unhappy, but because I wanted more (more impact, responsibility, growth, compensation, and learning as explained in Chapter 1). In one instance, I tried to increase my current team's power but failed at influencing my manager to make the proposed changes that would increase our power and therefore my engagement. I tried and failed; so, I moved on. I'm happy I made such moves as I plugged into teams working on things of high impact to the business and kept me engaged, challenged, and growing. Those moves enriched my career and life.

> Being in a team with relatively lower power is not the end of the world. There are ways to get in the right teams. If changing teams is not feasible for you, focus on increasing your relative power within your team by enhancing individual sources of power.

A Word of Caution

According to a negotiations professor I met, the risks of power include damaging relationships and creating conflict instead of collaboration. I would add that power can be misused or abused. Watch out for people who:

- Are low performers but extremely savvy political creatures. They lack substance, but they master the art of puckering up to kiss the right butts and so they are kept around somehow.
- Use power directly against you—I learned years later that a colleague actively blocked me from getting a promotion by raising a bogus concern with the executive panel, despite the fact I crushed it in the role, and I never had the chance to refute his claim.
- Abuse their power in unethical ways.

Listen, power, influence, and politics is not my favorite topic—I understand it well, but I don't master it—and playing it does not come naturally. But like Henry Kissinger alluded to in the chapter's opening quote, sheer competence is not enough! It really isn't. You need a healthy level of performance in this topic. Powerlessness can stunt your career growth you even if you have an enviable spike. You need to combine high performance with effective influence skills: The influence complements your abilities and helps convince others that your optimal idea is the winning one to implement. If you are successful enough to reach a position of power, use it wisely to help move the best ideas and people forward. Help give power the good rep it should have!

Wrap-Up

To get things done in your organization and career, you need to increase your power and gain allies. Yes, you can increase your power sources, both individual and contextual. Use your sources of power to advance the best ideas to the benefit of your organization, your career, and other people around you. You must reflect and determine where you currently land in The Road to Champagne power matrix, and then compare that to the level needed in your current position and the next one if you already have one in sight. Work your way closer to Race Car territory.

The measure of a man is what he does with power.
—Plato, Greek philosopher (approx. 427–347 BC)

Take-Aways: Increase Power and Influence

- Bad news for you: Competence in your role is not enough. You also need the ability to convince others to accept and implement your ideas.
- Power and influence make things happen in your organization, and you need to be aware of those dynamics.
- Power and influence make you a more effective professional and leader; therefore, build and develop effective levels of both.
- Yes, you can get to your Champagne faster in a race car! So work your way into one.

Self-Assessment

Which statement describes you best? Circle the corresponding letter.

a. Playing the power game is not for me, so I stay out of it. I have always believed my results and performance are all that matter.

b. I do pay attention to the power dynamics around me, but I am not that good at it. I haven't really studied it or practiced it enough.

c. For my role, I am adequately proficient at power, politics, and influence—it could even be a secondary spike. A healthy dose of influence complements my performance.

Actions

- Make sure you completed the power source assessment earlier in the chapter.
- Define concrete steps for each prioritized power source through a simple action plan.
    - What will you do? Be clear and include these actions in your calendar. Make them happen!

o By when? Set target dates and commit to the time and effort required.

<u>Target date:</u>

Power gap #1 to close: _____

Actions: _____ _____

                _____ _____

                _____ _____

                _____ _____

Power gap #2 to close: _____

Actions: _____ _____

                _____ _____

                _____ _____

                _____ _____

Power gap #3 to close: _____

Actions: _____ _____

                _____ _____

                _____ _____

                _____ _____

- Go deeper into the study of power and influence (books, courses, coaches, others).
- On an ongoing basis in your current role: When you face a key goal that you need to achieve, incorporate power into your planning. Ask and answer these questions:
  o What am I trying to achieve?

  _____

  _____

  o Who plays an important role for me to get there?

  _____

  _____

  o What are their interests and positions regarding my goal (blocker, neutral, or supporter)?

  _____

  _____

    o What power sources do they have?

    _____

    _____

    o What power sources do I currently have?

    _____

    _____

- Based on your power sources, their interests and positions, and their power sources, create a strategy outlining the steps you need to take to prevent blockers from blocking you and/ or gain the support of decision makers (for instance, explain how your goal is aligned with their interests, mitigate their concerns, and bring a powerful ally to the meeting).

    _____

    _____

    _____

- Execute your plan and learn from what worked well and what didn't. Keep practicing.
  - o What worked well? _____

    _____

  - o What didn't? _____

    _____

CHAPTER 11

Build Your Village

Networking is more about farming than it is about hunting.
—Ivan Misner, American entrepreneur and author

Why Should You?

It takes a village to ... no, not raise a child ... to be successful! Success doesn't come just because you are ready for it based on your solid track record, amazing resume, strong brand, and bright smile. You need an effective level of power and influence—as we just saw—plus a healthy and vibrant network inside and outside your organization (which also helps strengthen your position of power and your influence). David Steward, author of *Doing Business by The Good Book*, states: "A good reputation and a good network are among the most valuable assets a person can have. Why? Because it opens doors that provide immediate access to otherwise inaccessible people."[1]

Relationships don't necessarily guarantee you'll get what you want, but they open the door so your message can be heard; then it's totally up to you and your persuasion skills. For example, many times in my life, a contact opened the door for an interview. Then it's up to me to convince the audience that my value proposition will benefit their team and company —the offers came after the interview, but the interview might not have happened without the connection. I would have been just another resume in the messy stack.

Depending on the situation, in networking you will play one of three roles where a connector matches the needs of person A with the offering

---

[1] D.L. Steward. 2004. *Doing Business by The Good Book*. Hyperion.

of person B (or just A and B if no connector is needed). This creates a win-win-win scenario:

- Person A <u>needs</u> something such as good advice, a new job, widgets, and so on.
- Person B <u>possesses</u> something such as good advice, a job opening in their team, widgets, and so on.
- The successful connector puts A and B together for their gain, but also gains the appreciation of—and perhaps future reciprocity from—A and B.

The scenarios above highlight the multiple benefits if you have a strong network. It positions you to be an effective person A, person B, or connector. A partial list of your benefits includes:

- Better access to information necessary to achieve your goal (either in your current role or to change roles) because others are better positioned in the communications flow. Alternatively, if you are in a better communication flow position, you help others with the information they need.
- Increases your power and influence because you are associated with more powerful individuals (whatever their source of power is). Alternatively, if you are the one with relatively more power, you can help others achieve their goal.
- Provides a sounding board for ideas because others can share their perspectives with you, and vice versa.
- Provides you a sense of security because you are confident you have access to the right individuals who will give you a hand if you are ever in a time of need.
- More friendships! Who says all network relationships or interactions are business related? Many of my friends have provided sound professional advice, investment advice, or valuable restaurant recommendations when I visit their home country.

Good, we established that a good network has value and benefits. Now the tough part is building, maintaining, and expanding it because it requires time and effort—but worth every minute invested.

Establish Your Network

I know, this sounds scary if you are just getting started. But realize you already have a network. You are probably not starting from scratch (i.e., high school classmates, neighbors, college classmates, family, coworkers, and friends). However, your current network might not be robust enough to get you where you want to get.

But some people do start from scratch, especially if moving to a new country. That was the case of Neeraj Khanna, who told me in a podcast recording about his experience relocating from India to Ohio: "It started off being very difficult. I came to this country as a student—an undergraduate student ... first time in the U.S. And at that stage, it was all about starting from scratch—zero network, zero connections." He described that stage as "very daunting." Hopefully, you are not in such a challenging position as Neeraj was: But if you are, be confident it is possible to create a robust network over time. He did, and in doing so he has grown in the financial services industry to become a senior vice president at a leading bank.

In your network, you have four different types of contacts, as illustrated in Figure 11.1.

What differs between the four types is how strong the relationship is and therefore how active the communication flow is: From very frequent

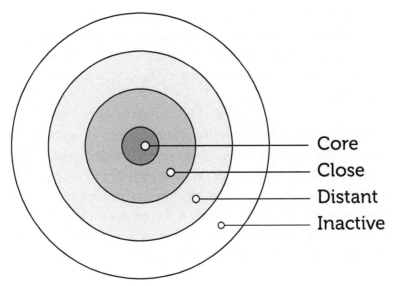

— Core
— Close
— Distant
— Inactive

Figure 11.1 Contact Types

and open to "OMG, it's been 15+ years!" Generally, you have fewer contacts the closer you are to the center. You must strategically figure out who you should bring toward the center. Sometimes, you should move some outwards if they are a negative influence on you (yes, relationship Spring cleaning). Some tips on each:

- Core: Make sure this group is diverse and includes people that can help you grow; thus, if you only have your high-school Beer Pong Club buddies here, you have some work to do. Include influential people inside and outside your organization.
- Close: Ensure diversity of backgrounds, industries, interests, and experience. This group might require more effort to maintain than Core contacts, because you might not interact organically with them anymore (ex-colleagues, for instance).
- Distant: This group is not less important than the first two. Often this is where you go for connections and information. Having a broad network will result in a large distant group. Identify who you need to bring in closer. Don't be shy to reach out to Distant contacts when needed, some will be pleasantly surprised and ready to help—although expect some will not bother to respond.
- Inactive: It's normal to have many dormant contacts, just make sure you don't have good people here out of laziness on your part—I know because I can plead guilty to that charge. Reach out to those you appreciate and make them Distant, at least.

Earlier in my career when I was less proficient at networking, I wrote in a business school paper "Sometimes I feel like 'why should I bother talking to that old bald guy with the little tie, I'd rather go home,' but I need to make a conscious effort." To this day, my introverted side tells me: *"Event is over, go home and read that book you started,"* but my extroverted side weighs in too and keeps me balanced: *"Go meet some new people or say hi to that person you met a few months ago."* I would be much better at it if I were more extroverted, but it just means I have to work a little harder than others. A friend explained to me how he is a natural at building and maintaining relationships. That is amazing and I'm jealous, because the rest of us have to be a little more strategic and methodic. And no offense to old bald guys—now I'm closer to the older crowd and not growing hair like before—my comment was more about the distracting little tie which is a quick fix!

In that business school paper I wrote, I listed advice to myself on how to actively start building my network when starting at Kearney after graduation: "Find out which people are powerful in your areas of interest (say Consumer Goods Practice), what activities they participate in, and join that team. Now make yourself visible and volunteer to assist them, build rapport, get them to know you (without overdoing it or being obvious)." Like any other goal, it requires planning and not random events of the universe. This advice implies a few actions on your part, as listed in Table 11.1

Table 11.1 Build Your Village action plan

Action	Description
Design your desired network	Know what *type* of contacts would bring value to your career—now or later. Think strategically about: <ul><li>Internal and external to your organization. You need both for performance and growth in your organization and you need external ones when it's time to leave your organization.</li><li>Inside and outside your industry or field. You need diversity of thought. For example, mine includes entrepreneurs, journalists, real estate agents, doctors, and others outside my corporate world.</li><li>All levels: More senior, peers, and more junior. Yes, more junior! Not only to mentor them, but they are great resources to help you with analytical tools and technology you don't master. Some will outgrow you if you select and mentor them well.</li></ul>
Assess gaps versus current network	Assess the gaps between your current and desired network. Identify the types of contact you need more of. This will depend on your field, goals, and current network.
Define your proposition	Be clear on what you can offer your network because it's not there just for your benefit. You will use this information to help kickstart relationships: Know how to offer your help in something they care about (i.e., making a connection, sharing an insight, and so on.)

(Continued)

Table 11.1 (Continued)

Create a plan	Create a plan to fill in the gap between your current and desired network:
	• List names of people that come to mind for each type of contact needed.
	• Learn about them: Interests, hobbies, alma maters, affiliations, commonalities.
	• Create intersections:
	  o Figure out who can introduce you.
	  o Attend meetings or events they attend, introduce yourself to them and others as well (others may be equally valuable, you never know).
	  o Share information that would benefit them (a contact or relevant insights).
	  o Offer to help them.
	  o Be creative.
	• Build genuine rapport and authentic interest in them. No one appreciates fake attempts to be befriended. Just because you are planful doesn't mean you can't be genuine.

Don't always plan	Take advantage of unplanned touchpoints. The plan above is for conscious gap-filling but be friendly and nice to all. Going to a cross-functional meeting? Introduce yourself to all and keep in touch. Some will be future project teammates.
Benchmark	Learn best practices. *"Identify the people in your organization who successfully achieve results and influence others. How well do you know and relate to these people? Find out how they leverage their networks."*[2]

Keep exercising this muscle. It takes time, effort, and dedication to build and grow your network throughout your career, but it is fun as well. I joined a group of local professionals who would meet for dinner periodically in a different restaurant, and the mix of people always changed: It created random exposure to people from all fields. Maintaining your network also requires discipline and time. Reach out to a set of different people every week, just check in and ask what's new via e-mail or LinkedIn message, perhaps offering a brief update of your recent achievements or news. If you do that at least once a year for Distant contacts, you will keep the relationship alive and will have a huge

---

[2] S.H. Gebelein et al. 2001. *Successful Manager's Handbook*. Personnel Decisions International.

advantage over most. Of course, Core and Close contacts should be seen, called, and texted more often.

Your network enriches your life too, it's not just about career goals. When I travel, I try to see friends and contacts in that city. For example, when I vacationed in Southeast Asia, I made a point to hang out with friends from Cornell, Kellogg, and Virginia. I went to Ben's family birthday party in Bangkok, had dinner with Heng in Kuala Lumpur, dinner at Klaus and Ley Cheng's in Singapore, and I became a city tour guide in Bangkok to don Hugo (whose son and daughters are our friends in Virginia) since I took him to sites he hadn't visited while he temporarily lived there for a project. Those meetups made my trip even more enjoyable.

You are tempted to forget the priceless relationships when all is well, and you are not in need … resist that temptation and always invest time in your network. Have you been contacted by ghostly voices from the past who have not been in touch, only to ask for a favor? It doesn't feel nice, does it? Let's avoid it. One way to minimize this is by identifying about 10 to 20 core connections that you believe would be critical to you when trying to:

- Obtain new information, insights, and best practices related to your field.
- Gain political support, resources, or mentorship.
- Hear unbiased developmental feedback and challenges to your ideas.
- Get personal support.
- Regain a sense of purpose and meaning.
- Improve work/life balance through physical well-being, spirituality, hobbies, and so on.
- Find an exciting opportunity if you were fired tomorrow.

The list above is from an HBR article[3] with the last point added by me. This summarizes well the roles fulfilled by a strong network.

---

[3] R. Cross, and R. Thomas. July–August 2011. "A Smarter Way to Network." *Harvard Business Review*.

Now, write their names ... yes now (think former bosses, head-hunters, executives, mentors, influential contacts in your field, family, friends, and so on.).

———————————, ———————————, ———————————,

———————————, ———————————, ———————————,

———————————, ———————————, ———————————,

———————————, ———————————, ———————————,

———————————, ———————————, ———————————,

———————————, ———————————, ———————————,

These are your VIPs; therefore, proactively reignite the flames of the relationship by being in touch periodically. Perhaps you can share a relevant article they would be interested in, share a recent accomplishment of yours, ask them how their family and business is doing, and if local, invite them for coffee or a drink. Do you know how much easier you will make it for them to help you when needed? I've outlined the basic elements of networking, but many books have been written because it is a rich topic. I encourage you to go deeper into it.

A key insight from my conversation with Neeraj is how he approaches networking: "Be genuine about the curiosity that you present in the conversation, be genuine about trying to learn about the other person and what they do, have that curiosity be a genuine curiosity. And listen." The optimal way to approach relationship-building is to be authentically interested in the other person, and to find a way to offer to help them before you even ask them for help.

> *You can make more friends in two months by becoming interested in other people than you can in two years by trying to get other people interested in you.*
> —Dale Carnegie, American writer and lecturer (1888–1955)

Key Relationships

Let's discuss mentors, coaches, sponsors, and other key relationships you must foster.

Mentors are people in your organization or network who have more experience and can guide you toward growth and success. They are typically more senior leaders who share their wisdom with you with the objective of steering, challenging, and supporting you. They act as advisers who want to see you succeed. Mentors help you navigate the internal political landscape, since they are more knowledgeable about how it operates. They also make their network (or select contacts) available to you.

In many organizations, there is a structured program where you are assigned to a mentor and/or a mentee. In most cases, it's totally up to you to make it happen. They are invaluable and you need them—not only to gain access to knowledge, advice, and seasoned perspectives related to your work, but also to help you think through career decisions. It is important to clarify mutual expectations upfront to maximize the probability of a value-added relationship: You want more out of it than a nice lunch every three months. Good questions they can help you think through include:

- How would you navigate this difficult situation I am in, if you were in a similar position?
- I don't think my relationship with the head of that department is as smooth as I would like it to be. Since you know him, what do you think I can do differently to enhance the relationship?
- I am thinking of moving to that team for these three reasons. Do you think that is a sensible move, given my long-term goal?

Remember Alex the Physicist? It was his mentor who challenged him to aim higher when thinking about which universities to apply to for a professor position. I've had many mentors: Some play that role for only a few years, others much longer. You will have turnover in your board of advisers, just make sure you do have a pool of three to five mentors helping you think and grow.

I would suggest you be upfront when talking to an executive about your interest in them considering being your mentor, but only after you have built a relationship. You want to make sure you don't place them in an awkward spot with such a request: A cold request can be a turn-off. And respect their decision, because at the end of the day, they will mentor who they want to mentor and you may not be it. I have mentored people as well, and it is just easier when you know each other, and have a genuine interest in their success.

> *Mentoring is a brain to pick, an ear to listen, and a push in the right direction.*
> —John C. Crosby, American politician (1859–1943)

Gebelein et al. explain, "Coaching is the process of equipping people with the tools, knowledge, and opportunities they need to develop themselves. Effective coaches are catalysts who make development quicker and more effective."[4] A coach is different from a mentor. It's not a senior executive in your organization. It can be your manager, a coworker, or even a professional career coach. A coach can help you overcome a development area that is hindering you from growth. You work with a coach to improve that specific point, and when you achieve it, the coaching is no longer needed. Good questions they can address include:

- How can I overcome my shyness when public speaking?
- What can I do to enhance my executive presence?
- How can I become more proficient at using this software?

When I onboarded two new managers reporting to me at RBI, I acted as a coach until they became independent, because they were new to the industry and company. I helped them learn what they needed to do to succeed in the role, and given their drive and intelligence, that phase went by quickly. Then I stepped back and got out of their way.

Another objective for coaching is laying out a plan to achieve a career aspiration (mentors will give advice, but they won't get into the details of creating a plan for you). This is the focus of career coaches, of course. During my Cadbury days, I worked with Pat, a career coach, who helped me think about my future path alternatives and to create a

---

[4] S.H. Gebelein et al. 2001. *Successful Manager's Handbook.* Personnel Decisions International.

plan for getting there (what skills to refine or acquire, for instance). He helped me think through critical career questions. Depending on where you are in your journey, and what areas you need to improve, consider a career coach.

You should coach more junior people around you. Invest in their development and use your areas of strength to help them overcome their developmental areas. Or, leverage your network and pair up Sammy who needs to refine a certain skill with Joe who is a guru at it. Give back and use your network to help.

A crucial relationship to seek, for advancing to senior levels, is a sponsor. A sponsor advocates for you, to help you progress in your journey within the organization: He or she uses his or her power and influence to ensure you are considered for promotions and key roles and provides brutal feedback. They can influence the direct decision maker(s). Having the right sponsor(s) is game-changing. If you do, consider yourself fortunate, and it is a sign you are checking all or most boxes (performance, reputation, others).

According to Sylvia Ann Hewlett, author of *(Forget a Mentor) Find a Sponsor*, "it's the secret sauce, the missing link, the invisible dynamic that accounts for who is and who isn't, in power." [5] The rationale is simple: to get to the coveted senior positions you need to be *pulled in* from the inside … you can't just deliver results and magically be invited to join the coveted leadership team. You must cultivate a strategic alliance with someone high enough to make it happen. I suggest diving deeper into this topic, perhaps starting with relevant books.

> It is tough to get invited to be part of your organization's executive team. It is exponentially tougher to achieve it without a sponsor who convinces others to invite you in.

Besides mentors, coaches, and sponsors, there are other key relationships you need depending on your context. Identify them. For example,

---

[5] S.A. Hewlett. 2013. *(Forget a Mentor) Find a Sponsor*. Harvard Business Review Press.

in consulting firms, there is one person in charge of project staffing for that office: Bringing the right people to the right project. At Kearney, I established a good relationship with her, and I reminded her of my interests, skills, and development goals. Instead of being informed about my next project, she would ask me for my preference between options. She once offered the postmerger integration project at Cadbury in New Jersey, or a project with L'Oreal in New York City. I chose Cadbury given my food background, and still wonder how my life would have shaped had I chosen L'Oreal. That presented an unknown but significant fork in the road, and she let me choose because we had a good working relationship.

Relationships Work

I am not a master networker. I would consider myself average relative to peers and I must continue to improve. Average relative to my peers is still relatively decent though. It requires effort to maintain it, and even more to grow it. Of course, my network has grown over time, as should yours. Different affiliations gave me instant access to established networks (i.e., my schools and ex-companies) and living in several cities has helped me multiply it from a professional and social perspective.

Let me illustrate how the power of networks and relationships have helped me throughout my career, starting at business school.

- Kellogg to Kearney: As I mentioned in Chapter 4, I joined Kearney as a summer intern. Based on my performance, I later received an offer to join full-time in Alexandria VA, after graduation. However, due to macroeconomic circumstances that year, my start date got delayed three months. Because I did not want to sit around accumulating bills with no income, I contacted many local Kellogg alumni I did not know. Many did not respond, but Mark, the CFO of his company, did and he offered me a three-month consulting gig and even paid me more than Kearney.

- Kearney to Cadbury New Jersey: While at Kearney,
  I had a project with Cadbury—I helped orchestrated
  the integration of Cadbury and Adams manufacturing
  networks with hundreds of plants across the world. I got
  to create close relationships with my client team, even
  traveling together to five continents. I enjoyed the work
  that we were doing. They asked me to join them full
  time and offered to start my green card process—which
  I needed—so I did.
- Cadbury New Jersey to Cadbury South America: I expressed
  my interest to join his team directly to Marcos, the president
  of Cadbury South America. A few months later I relocated
  to join his team.
- Cadbury South America to McKinsey: After deciding to
  leave Cadbury after the acquisition by Kraft, I contacted two
  partners at Kearney in the United States because I became
  interested in joining Kearney in São Paulo. They introduced
  me to a local partner, and I had the offer after interviewing.
  However, one of the Kearney interviewers recommended I
  talk to McKinsey before accepting, because several of his colleagues had left to join McKinsey. He introduced me to them,
  I interviewed, got an offer, and I accepted after weighing the
  pros and cons of both offers.
- McKinsey to Restaurant Brands International (RBI): I spoke
  to two close McKinsey partners in Miami to let them know
  I decided it was my time to leave and asked if they knew
  of local opportunities. Both wanted to help. Luis sent my
  resume to Paulo, a McKinsey alum at RBI looking for talent
  for his team. I spoke to Paulo, he asked me to interview, and
  I soon joined his team.
- RBI to Southern Glazer's Wine & Spirits (SGWS): When
  I searched for new opportunities in Miami, I reached out
  to my ex-Kearney colleague Lawrence. He put me in touch
  with his former boss at SGWS, Stephen. Stephen invited
  me to interview with him and with his team. I did, and later
  joined them.

None of those moves were done by responding to job postings online or answering a recruiter's call. All those doors opened because either I had a relationship with someone where I wanted to go, or with someone who knew someone there. To minimize risks of costly hiring errors, decision makers want to hire people they know and trust, or people that are vouched for by people they trust.

Do you get why I am advocating strongly for you to build a good net-work (plus a strong brand)? It opens doors! My aforementioned examples focus on career moves, but the principle also applies internally within our organization. Knowing who to contact to provide expertise or remove an obstacle is key in getting stuff done. More than a decade ago, I built a probabilistic financial model and needed to run the model 1,000 times to capture a histogram of the financial outcome to determine what percent-age of the time the project was attractive, and a simple macro would do that quickly. I didn't know how to build the macro, so I contacted Cristina in Brazil, who worked with me in an earlier project, and she efficiently built the macro for me. Voilà!

> You and I don't need to know how to do everything, just who to call.

Very importantly, my relationships have also allowed me to open doors for others. Recently, Carlos, an ex-colleague, contacted me inter-ested in a posted Director role for my team. Because I knew he had the right profile and a great reputation, I connected him with my boss and the recruiter. I endorsed him (which I only do when certain), stepped away, and let Carlos do his thing during the interview process. He's my coworker again.

Taylor, my ex-colleague and buddy from the Iceland trip, also searched for new opportunities. I was aware that Tony, an executive I worked with internally, needed a VP of Commercial Strategy. Knowing Taylor's ex-McKinsey capabilities and strong performance, I introduced them and now he's again my coworker. These are a couple of recent examples to stress that the power of your network and relationships must be used to help others too—it's not just about how others can help you. Keep it balanced that way.

Wrap-Up

To be effective in your current role, and in your career, not only do you need power and influence as explained in the previous chapter, you need to have the right relationships. It is critical to cultivate authentic and long-term relationships—undoubtedly it will help your career and life. This is how Neeraj approaches it. Do not form relationships simply to take advantage of people's privileged positions. The good news is you already have an existing network. Figure out what improvements are needed based on your goals and create a plan to make it happen. "Your success is exponential if you can leverage a network," said Neeraj. You also have an obligation to help others, you shouldn't just seek to be helped by your network. Invest the time and effort needed to build, maintain, and expand your network and you will see amazing benefits come to you and those you help.

> *What makes networking work is that it sets up win-win situations in which all parties involved get to take something home. Networking is a sharing process. Until you understand that, you won't have much of a network.*
> —Earl G. Graves, Sr., American entrepreneur and publisher
> (1935–2020)

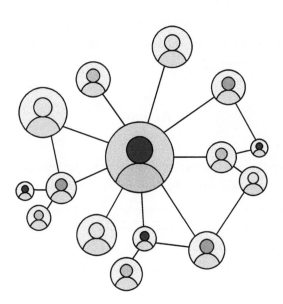

Take-Aways: Build Your Village

- Your growth, opportunities, and success happen because others are willing to trust you.
- Relationships open doors in your life.
- Invest time and effort in building and maintaining your network when you don't need something from it.
- Always have a group of three to five mentors. Use coaches as needed. Do not overlook the criticality of at least one sponsor.
- Give back! Mentor some, coach some, be a sponsor if you are already up there, and use your network to help others.

Self-Assessment

Which statement describes you best? Circle the corresponding letter.

a. My network has many holes like Swiss cheese, when compared to the ideal network I should have for my role and the future success I envision for me. Building relationships is not my thing.

b. My network is good. I have the right type of contacts, but I need to be more strategic about expanding it. I need to be more proactive at keeping existing relations alive.

c. I built an internal and external network suited for my role and future growth ambition. I am well connected: My network helps me—and others—achieve goals. I am a mentee and a mentor.

Actions

<u>Networking</u>
- Assess the gaps between your current and desired network. What *types* of contacts do you need more of?
  - a) _____
  - b) _____
  - c) _____
  - d) _____
  - e) _____

- Create a plan to fill in the gap between your current and desired network:
  - List names of people that come to mind for each type of contact needed.
    a) _____, _____ , _____
    b) _____, _____ , _____
    c) _____, _____ , _____
    d) _____, _____ , _____
    e) _____, _____ , _____
  - Create intersections. How will you connect with them, given what you know of them?
    a) _____
    b) _____
    c) _____
    d) _____
    e) _____
- Define what you can offer these new contacts that they would value:
  - _____
  - _____
  - _____

Sponsor, Mentor and Coach

- Identify who—in a position of power—can become your sponsor(s). Figure out how you can help them and engage them in a conversation to share why such relationship would be mutually beneficial.
  - _____
  - _____
- Identify three to five potential mentors; People you already know inside and outside your organization:
  - _____
  - _____
  - _____
  - _____
  - _____

- Get closer to them. At the right time, invite them to consider establishing such a relationship.
- If they accept, clarify mutual expectations including frequency of dialogue.
- Identify one or two people you are willing to mentor and start the dialogue:
    - _____
    - _____
- Determine what areas you need to develop (perhaps based on recent feedback or performance reviews per Chapter 6):
    - _____
    - _____
    - _____
- Identify proficient contacts in those topics that your trust and believe they are willing to help you:
    - _____, _____, _____
    - _____, _____, _____
    - _____, _____, _____
- Ask them if they would help you by providing coaching in that topic.
- Agree on the objective, approach, and what success looks like.
- Identify one or two people you are willing to coach on a given topic you master and offer 30 minutes or so a week for coaching:
    - _____
    - _____

CHAPTER 12

Grab the Wheel

The people who get on in this world are the people who get up and look for the circumstances they want, and, if they can't find them, make them.

—George Bernard Shaw, Irish playwright and Nobel Prize winner (1856–1950)

Why Should You?

I am a car aficionado. I love fast cars, sexy-looking cars, and hearing a powerful engine roar is the only music I need. I took one exhilarating class many years ago: The two-day BMW M-School, a high-performance driving course. The class of about 20 fellow car nuts spent those days learning driving skills from professional drivers and practicing out on the track. It was exhilarating to sit behind the wheel of many BMW M cars, including my favorite: The M5. I felt the rush when in control of a high-powered monster roaring through the track and getting it to do exactly what I wanted.

That should be your exact goal: To get behind the wheel of your career and life and help steer it in the desired direction—toward your Champagne ... whatever that exciting goal is. When opportunities don't come to you as we discussed in Chapter 4, you must seek, pursue, or create your own opportunities.

Do not waste your time waiting for others to bring opportunities to you because you will likely be disappointed by the lack of action or the quality of the opportunity. Many people are passive and wait for others to make it happen for them. They hope their boss, or HR partner, or mentors will surprise them with exciting news, but that is not how it works. Your lovely boss is not prioritizing moving roadblocks for your career growth, he or she is probably busy thinking about the roadblocks they need to move for their own growth ... not yours. Besides, given your newly sharpened self-awareness, only you can factually understand what projects or roles are ideal—those that leverage your strengths and interests, allow you to enhance areas of development, sharpen your professional brand, and better position you to achieve your long-term goals. For example, I reported to someone who wanted me to take a global procurement role based in Switzerland because that is how he needed to beef-up his team, but I had no interest, neither in that role nor in the location—at that time or to this day.

You will be disappointed if you rely on others to properly manage your career. It is exclusively your responsibility, so start taking control of it now. Do not delegate the management of your career to anyone, because when you delegate—or are not proactive enough—the potential outcomes are the following:

- Surprise ... nothing happens.
- Something happens, but not fully aligned with the direction you envisioned.
- It happens, but it took too long.
- Wow ... it happens as expected.

I have no scientific research to prove my next point, but I would safely assume it's directionally correct: The probability of each of those outcomes materializing is already in descending order. My guess is 70-20-7-3 percent.

Let me share an extreme example of being passive. Many years ago, a friend from church told me she needed a job, so she was praying for it. That's awesome, I thought, so I asked her what else she was doing to find such job. She responded she was *only* praying for it. I probably scratched my head. Since I believe our faith must be matched with action, in her shoes I would have wrangled my network, found out who knows someone in my target companies, ensured I have the skills for that desired position, and so on. I shared with her James 2:17; "In the same way, faith by itself, if it is not accompanied by action, is dead." I explained to her why when I pray for something, I am certain God wants me to also roll up my sleeves and work at it!

What concerns me is that I've met too many people who are passively waiting on something to happen; They want more, but they sit passively waiting on a miracle from God, lucky stars, or their HR team. "If it's meant to be, it will be," they say. That is a nice phrase for situations you have no control over or don't really care about the outcome; But it's certainly not a robust career management strategy. If you want an envisioned outcome to materialize, you must work to make it happen!

The Two-Step Approach

"So, Alejandro, how can I become more proactive at managing my career? How do I make it happen?" Glad you asked. There are two main steps:

1. Define what you want.
2. Go for it.

That's it. I don't have a complex answer for you. OK, OK, it's not as simple, so let's explore each step.

Step 1. First, you need to know what you want. What you want should be related to many principles we explored in the previous chapters. You need to know what you want more of and where to get it—while aiming high and being adaptable. This should also position you to acquire experiences that contribute to the brand you are constructing and be aligned with your values.

To define this, you should do some introspection, explore and assess different potential paths (within your organization and outside), speak to different people closer to those paths, get advice from your trusted board of mentors, and perhaps design your future job description if such role does not yet exist in your organization.

I must confess, sometimes I struggle with this first step. Sometimes it takes me longer than desired to define my next move. But once I know, I fully dive into the second step, which is much easier for me.

Don't get close to step 2 until step 1 is very clear.

Step 2. Once you defined that path, you are ready to go for it. But don't rush it, though, because you need to *plan* before you *execute*. To plan your path to that next growth phase:

- **Define who to talk to.** These are people that can pull you in or open that door. Perhaps the leader of that team. Or someone that is close to the leader of your team of interest. Hopefully, these are people you already have a relationship with. If you don't have a relationship, you must start from the relationship-building stage which as you know, takes time. There are no shortcuts though; You need to have some level of relationship with the decision makers (or influence over them, which is tougher).

- **Synthesize your message** around why you want to join them and why they want you to be part of their team; In other words, why they want to accept your proposal. Appeal to their interests, show how your proposal helps them and not only your career growth. They don't care about your needs, it's about what you can do for them and what value you bring to them. This includes showcasing your main spike(s), track record of results, unique skills they need, and so forth. Your goal is to make them realize they are incomplete without you … literally.

- **Determine how to approach them** (i.e., when to do it, where to do it, and how the conversation should flow). Tactical stuff, but important, nonetheless. Be strategic about the tactics by ensuring the conversations happen when they are not stressed or rushed, in a place with few interruptions, in a fashion that get them interested in supporting you, with the right sequence of arguments, showcasing some evidence if needed, and so forth.

Once I figure out the design, I do not waste time and I promptly execute the plan. I meet with those I need to speak with, and I expose them to my interests and the reasons why they are also interested in opening such door for me. More often than not, it works! If you did your home-work well (i.e., defined a logical next move, designed the approach well, and executed it according to plan), you will plant a seed in their minds and they will eventually open that door for you. It becomes a win–win proposition, not an unwelcomed request for a favor.

Different people struggle with either or both steps, while some for-tunate ones don't have difficulties with either. Do you struggle with any? Which one? _____ It's better to struggle with these two steps because it's uncomfortable to go through them, than to not struggle because you are not going through them.

I urgently motivate you to be proactive and take matters into your own hands. Fight for what you want more of … make it happen. Grab the wheel and start steering. Don't be passive. Don't be like those who sit on their hands in the back seat waiting for someone to drive them around: They won't get far. The following stories illustrate what grabbing the wheel looks like.

> *A wise man will make more opportunities than he finds.*
> —Francis Bacon, English philosopher and
> statesman (1561–1626)

Burning the Ships

As I told you earlier, at some point in my Cadbury life while in New Jersey, I became a little bored and wanted exciting changes and new experiences. Remember I told you in Chapter 3 I had become super intrigued and interested in living in Brazil, when exposed to Portuguese and *capoeira* lessons? Brazil was the place to be around that time, since it was one of the four emerging economies known as BRIC (Brazil, Russia, India, China).

I had a business trip coming up to visit our South American team based in São Paulo. I contacted a colleague in Brazil and asked him to share with me information related to the recently created strategic roadmap for the South America business unit that they shared with our CEO. Then, I e-mailed Dani, the executive assistant to the South America president, and asked her for 20 minutes with Marcos. She promptly replied asking

me what for. I explained I wanted to express my interest in joining Marcos'
team. She must have discussed it with him, and she later e-mailed, "I will
make it a one-hour lunch."

Finally, the day arrived, sometime in March. The office did not have a
cafeteria, so they set a table for us in the large balcony overlooking Avenida
Paulista, one of the iconic avenues of the city. In Portuguese, I explained
to Marcos that with my skills and experiences, I could help him with
three out of his five strategic priorities. I shared my resume with him and
gave him an overview of my background. He told me that many people
from the United States contacted him over the years expressing interest in
coming down to Brazil but none of them had made the effort to learn
Portuguese. I think he appreciated the fact that I did my homework to
understand the key concerns and priorities in his head and that I clearly
expressed how I would add value to his pursuits. My self-awareness made
me realize I would not be a good fit for two of the five strategic priorities,
but those three … heck yeah. We had a great conversation and lunch, and
I felt he welcomed my message.

A few months later in late July, I was taking an executive education
course on Mergers and Acquisitions at Wharton in Philadelphia. I worked
in postmerger integration and wanted to learn more about this highly
relevant topic.

> By the way, I asked my boss' boss to help fund that course, but he
> declined. So, I decided to pay for it myself. If you are not willing to
> invest in your education and development, who will?

While at Wharton, my phone rang and it was Carlos, the Head of
South America Supply Chain who reported to Marcos. He said "We
would like to invite you to come down to Brazil for two to three months
to help create the strategy for how we can enter the chocolate market
in Brazil, from an operations perspective. Can you come in the next
few weeks in mid-August?" Yes! I hung up and told Guilherme, a new
Brazilian friend I met at the course, "Hey, I'll be seeing you more often!"

The most likely outcome for anyone in that position is to pack a bag
for a two to three-month trip, right? That's the time period they invited me

for. But my self-confidence mixed with faith that this was the right move, led me to a different approach. I immediately called my wife and told her "Start selling our cars, pack everything, and sell the house. We're moving to Brazil!" In the second half of August, I bought a *one-way* ticket to São Paulo. My wife stayed behind and took care of all the selling arrangements.

The first day I showed up to the office to meet my new colleagues, I met Vini who co-led the commercial aspects of our project. He asked "So, are you a chocolate expert?" I laughed because the answer wasn't anything but a straight-up "No, but I am a chocolate lover." The skills I brought we're not about chocolate, I would pick up that product knowledge with him as we dove into the project.

By week six, I defined and assessed the strategic alternatives for how we should enter the chocolate market, including importing from other countries, creating a new local production plant, outsourcing local manufacturing, plus several hybrid options. I presented the pros, cons, and implications of each alternative to Marcos and his leadership team and explained my recommendation for the optimal solution. After the meeting, the executive team approached me and asked me to stay in Brazil and lead the execution phase of my strategy over the next few years. Little did they know I had already planted both feet in Brazil, and my wife was arriving the following week for good, after selling our house.

I pulled an Hernan Cortes move; Burning the ships that would take me back home if I failed at my mission, and thus eliminating failure as an option.[1] I understood that to achieve my goal of being invited to stay for years, I needed to do a spectacular job at my short-term mission and make them see me as a critical player to the success of the project, or risk returning to New Jersey with my tail between my legs, crushed dreams, to start looking for a new home.

Disclaimer: Please weigh the downsides if you ever want to imitate Hernan Cortes!

---

[1] R.H.Innes. 1998. "Hernan Cortes." *Britannica.* www.britannica.com/biography/Hernan-Cortes (accessed July 2020)

Our five-and-a-half years in Brazil were amazing (with Cadbury/ Mondelēz and then McKinsey) and that specific project remains one of the most engaging, entrepreneurial, fun, and fulfilling stages in my career. Marcos, Carlos, Oswaldo, and the rest of the former Cadbury South America team welcomed me and my wife and allowed us to make Brazil our third home. Burning the ships was well worth it.

Nothing ever happens in your life unless you create the space for it to happen in.

—James McCay, Australian actor

Sampa Housing

Lili Ferrarase lived in our same building in São Paulo. I liked that she had a noticeable international flair and genuinely connected to foreigners like us. Lili had an admired corporate job at JLL Hotels, given her degree in hotel management. She worked as an adviser to hotel developers and traveled to nice resorts throughout South America as part of her job, making many jealous, including me.

Years before I met her, the travel bug bit her and she wanted to move to Europe. Her manager mentioned that the Ireland office looked for someone with her profile and offered to make the connection: She replied *"Yes!"* She interviewed for the one-year assignment, got it, and moved to Dublin.

A year went by, and she was supposed to return to São Paulo. But it went too fast and she wanted to stay in Europe longer. When she was exploring KPMG's website searching for more information about a golf course development conference she was attending, she found an attractive position in their career page ... in Hungary. She proactively contacted the hiring manager via LinkedIn, who came back with next steps for an interview. Soon after, she started working for KPMG in Budapest.

Lili searched for a place to rent, and her experience with the rental process became extremely frustrating given the unappealing and unfriendly websites in Hungarian. Fortunately, a local realtor helped her find an amazing corporate apartment with a beautiful view of the Danube River, and made the rental process easy—it can be stressful and burdensome for a foreigner that doesn't speak the language. Lili later returned to São Paulo for family reasons, and JLL welcomed her back … that's when we met.

Lili lived in our building with her brother Ricky, who later moved to their parents' house in a different part of the city. To replace Ricky with a new apartment mate, she placed an ad on a website for expats. She was overwhelmed with so many responses! She selected her new apartment mate but remained intrigued by the huge demand. Remember, this was when being in Brazil was especially attractive, and many foreign professionals from Europe, North America, and Latin America were flocking to it.

I can confirm how painful the rental process was, with requirements such as having a guarantor that promises the landlord full financial guarantees on behalf of the tenant. When you move to a new country, how are you supposed to get a local guarantor if you don't know anyone? Nobody knows you or trusts you! When I first attempted to rent an apartment in that building, the owner wanted a letter from the "owner of Cadbury in London" which is absurd. After four or five long weeks of contract negotiations, the lawyers decided to abort, and that threw me back to square one. Fortunately, my real estate agent told me "I own the apartment just below this one, on the 26th floor, and I can rent it to you without the letter because I now know you and trust you." Lili and I understood the pain foreigners felt.

Back to Lili. She saw the opportunity and decided to rent a three-bedroom apartment in a nearby building and sublet each bedroom in the expat site. Interested tenants flooded her with requests, again! She furnished the place and rented it out to foreigners looking for a simple process, a nice apartment in a nice neighborhood, and the experience of living with other foreigners. Remembering her own frustrations in Budapest, Lili made the process easier by eliminating the red tape and guarantor requirement, and even allowing payment via credit card (typically you need to deposit money in the landlord's bank account and send proof of deposit). She created an innovative and disruptive business model which grew fast due to the huge demand.

After managing 15 apartments, Lili and her boyfriend Alex decided to quit their corporate jobs and manage the new business full-time. Lili wanted more learning, control, excitement, and entrepreneurial experience. The business evolved as it grew, from focusing on individual foreigners to focusing on the companies that brought their expat employees. Six years after launching Sampa Housing, they were managing 700 apartments in São Paulo! They sold the business in 2016, staying with the acquiring company for about two years to ensure a successful transition.

> By the way, the mother of Lili's boyfriend later kindly became our guarantor for an apartment we rented when I moved to be closer to the McKinsey office … the bureaucracy brings back goosebumps.

Lili explained to me that "It felt amazing to be in the driver's seat." She went from the comfort and stability of a corporate job to the hectic entrepreneur's life that sacrifices weekends, nights, vacations, and sleep. When asked what kept her going, she replied, "Hunger to learn more kept me going. I learned more in the first year than in ten years in my corporate role." Lili's story brings to life many principles in this book, and I wanted to showcase an entrepreneur's example for those that are pondering such a route. Lili is now sleeping well in her home near a beach in Portugal, with Alex and their little girls.

Thanks, But No Thanks

In 2009, Kraft expressed intentions to buy Cadbury to create the world's biggest confectioner, but the Cadbury Board of Directors had no interest and declined such offers. Such a deal would be devastating to the project I've been focused on for the past year-and-a-half because in Brazil, Kraft was the number one chocolate player with about 35 percent market share. It would not make sense to continue with our project that aimed to attack Kraft. But we were safe … until January 2010 when we received the surprising news that the Board accepted the deal. We agreed to abort all further efforts related to our project, and we did.

The start of production at the chosen manufacturing plant was only nine days away and we negotiated with suppliers to return the raw materials we bought but wouldn't need anymore. It was a horrible feeling. We worked for a year-and-a-half to create what would have been an excellent product portfolio for a successful market launch and were forced to kill it two inches from the goal line.

For the next several months, I changed my focus to help with the merger integration efforts, which is obviously a temporary endeavor. I immediately went from being employed by Cadbury South America to Kraft Brazil. I felt optimistic in my ability to find a new role to continue adding value to the newly merged organization. I thought about my next ideal role in this new world, given my strengths, interests (including staying in Brazil longer), and company needs. I concluded that an internal consulting team made sense for Kraft Brazil to achieve its strategic priorities and would allow me to deliver material value to the business. Next, I created a well-structured presentation outlining the quantitative and qualitative benefits of such a team, its setup, operating model, scope, organizational structure design, and why I should lead it. I created a superbly laid out proposal and I shared it with members of the new leadership team.

I did what I had to do: Envision the best outcome for me and try to convince others of it. But they showed no interest. It did not work. A silent "Thanks, but no thanks!" Fine, now I had more information to guide my decision-making process. In the absence of an exciting role in a new company, I decided to charter my own path and return to management consulting in Brazil. The message of this story is that sometimes the door you knock on will not open, but you won't know until you try. Will it stop me or you from continuing to knock on doors? Of course not. One thing is for sure, though: The likelihood of a desired door opening without you knocking on it is very close to zero.

Landing a Shark

When Dr. Juan Salinas was 12 years old, his dad wanted him to join the local swimming team in Honduras. But Juan had other plans: To improve his Atari skills. His dad insisted, telling him to try it for a month and then he could do as he pleased. Juan agreed (remember Principle 4?). Little did he know his first day at the pool would change his life by unleashing his new passion for sports and nutrition—one that is alive decades later. He went on to compete internationally with the national team.

At age 16, he relocated to the United States to immerse in the study of the English language so he could get proficient and apply to a university in the United States. His family taught him the value of education early on. That might explain why he pursued multiple degrees, including his Bachelor, Masters, PhD, and MBA at Rutgers University followed by the postgraduate diploma in sports and exercise nutrition (talk about Principles 3 and 8). His expertise was in product development, applying his abilities at leading food companies such as Nabisco, Cadbury (where we met), Kraft, and Nestlé. At Nestlé, he was a Global Project Director working on PowerBar. Despite enjoying developing relevant products for his employers, he lacked the conviction that the products he was developing were indeed "good for you" or healthy.

This created an itch to explore going his own way to launch a truly healthy snack. He realized he lacked the necessary business skills and therefore decided to obtain his MBA. This is a key step in taking control of your career: Not being static, especially if you feel you want more (more passion, conviction, and autonomy in Dr. Juan's case). The alternative is to bask in the stillness of career inertia. Dr. Juan realized his current job—and possibly career path—was not fulfilling and he acted on it. He even turned down a tempting offer to join another leading food company as R&D Director of Innovation with a fast track to VP, because it could have been more of the same.

The first product he developed was a complete disaster: A protein gel snack he never could successfully scale-up beyond his kitchen. He researched and experimented with new formats to deliver a similar concept but with less manufacturing issues. That's how he came across the extruded puff (think Cheetos). The development was harder than expected but he persevered.

In business school, he focused on entrepreneurship. He won first place in the annual business plan competition for his work to launch a healthy peanut-based snack: P-nuff Crunch. He also got a boost of confidence that his idea had potential. Dr. Juan kept working on this idea and eventually launched his product in the U.S. market. The same logic of his first day at the pool drove him to leave the corporate life and start his own business; "That week when I was making a decision to start my own business, I said to myself … 'Try it and if I don't like it or it doesn't work out then I can stop and go back to corporate or do something else. But you have to try,'" he explained.

Although the product had all the attributes needed for success, his sales were still modest a few years after launch, mostly due to limited distribution. That is when he decided to apply to Shark Tank, the famous ABC show where entrepreneurs pitch to the investors or sharks (Principles 1 and 2 at play). He did not hear anything for two years. But then he did. "They finally called and said 'Hey, we love your product and would love to see if you are interested in coming to the show to pitch to the Sharks?' and I was like … hell yeah!" he explained to me in my podcast with excitement and a burst of laughter. Fast-forward a bit and Dr. Juan succeeded at obtaining financing for his Perfect Life Nutrition company through a partnership with Mark Cuban.

Reflecting on his life as an employee, Dr. Juan said "I was waiting for management to reward me for my hard work as opposed to me talking to management and expressing myself about my wants and needs and what I was doing, and start to network in the company and get noticed." He added, "Don't expect people to do anything for you." Don't wait on others, be proactive in making your next career move happen whether internal or external.

Latin America and Caribbean

My first role at Restaurant Brands International was internally focused. My two main responsibilities were rolling out and embedding Problem-Solving Methodologies (PSM) and leading the Management by Objectives (MBO) process globally. Embedding PSM involved training and coaching employees and franchisees on how to use a better framework for addressing the different functional business issues they faced every day. MBO is about setting the individual goals for every employee in every function and region, cascaded down from the CEO's seven to ten goals for that year. At the end of each year, everybody would be assessed against their MBO plan achievement and their bonus would be objectively and mathematically calculated. This helps drive meritocracy, a key pillar of that corporate culture.

PSM and MBO were perfect platforms for me to contribute from day one, learn more about how the company operated, and gave me exposure to projects and executives across all functions and regions. But I always saw that as an entry point into the company.

I started thinking about my next role. I coached a project manager who worked for the head of global operations, Rodrigo. During those months I interacted frequently with Rodrigo. I liked our interactions and his no-nonsense, down-to-Earth, empowering leadership style, plus the type of work his team did. It was also evident he liked me and my work. I brought this up with my manager, not only to keep him informed but to gain his support for my potential future move. I expressed no urgency: Whenever the right time arrived.

One day, I spoke to Rodrigo and I told him that at the right time, I would be certainly interested in joining his team because I enjoyed working with him. He welcomed my interest, we agreed to explore it in the future, we shook hands and went back to work.

A couple of months later, Rodrigo became the new president of Latin America and Caribbean. Shortly after, my boss called me to a meeting in a conference room on a different floor. When I walked in, I saw him and Rodrigo. They told me I was promoted into a role reporting to Rodrigo, as Head of Supply Chain and Procurement for Latin America and Caribbean. That was an exciting move because it changed my focus from internal to external, while moving me to a team where the action is (i.e., with more power).

Now I dealt with suppliers across the Americas, all the franchisees in dozens of countries, plus many different functions within the organization. I love working with diverse countries across the Americas, and this role gave me another opportunity to visit many of them and interact with all of them, which was an unexpected benefit I ignored when I expressed interest to Rodrigo.

I applied my previous knowledge of process improvement, PSM, negotiations, and operations, to help turn around this function into a highly efficient and effective one and bring concrete savings to the franchisees (through the work of all my team, obviously). Had I not actively expressed my interest directly to the person that I became interested in working for, perhaps I'd land somewhere else not as fulfilling, engaging, and dynamic.

Wrap-Up

Lili and Juan made things happen in their lives. I have never relied on HR or my boss to make my next step happen. I involve them, but I have never let them drive the process for me. One HR executive once told me that career management was not a responsibility of his HR Talent Management team … it was my responsibility. I must admit it shocked me a bit, but it's true. Isn't HR there to help talented individuals grow? Not exactly. Don't fool yourself waiting for things to happen in your career just because you're delivering great results … expecting others to move the chess pieces for you. It is your responsibility to proactively build the right relationships, make your interests be known, knock on doors, take the right risks, and make things happen for yourself.

Have a career plan, understand what your next step should be, and work toward it. Remember that you need flexibility to adjust as needed. Being the driver is about better controlling the direction—and pace—of your career. Dr. Juan Salinas shared a spot-on reminder, "Make sure that you are following your passion during that time that we have. It's not a long time, so why waste it on things you want to do or that you have to do because you got stuck in a job and you feel like you are trapped. Get out of it! Go and do the things you really want to do." Don't get trapped, want more, and work to make it happen.

> *If you're proactive, you don't have to wait for circumstances or other people to create perspective-expanding experiences. You can consciously create your own.*
> —Stephen Covey, American bestselling author (1932–2012)

Take-Aways: Grab the Wheel

- Before you knock on the door(s) you want, do your home-work, and prepare: Some will open, some will not.
- To improve your career and life, you must believe in yourself and take educated risks.
- Be 100 percent committed to an outcome, remove failure from being an option.
- Never wait for others to make it happen for you. It's on you!

Self-Assessment

Which statement describes you best? Circle the corresponding letter.

a. I've always trusted the system: I let my boss and HR figure out what my next move should be. If it's meant to happen, it will!

b. I am neither passive nor proactive. I do talk to decision makers about my growth desires, but I don't create a plan B. If nothing happens … hey, at least I tried!

c. I proactively and strategically engage the right people to help me get to my desired next stage. If I do not see progress or growth arrive, I strive to make it happen.

Actions

- Step 1. Think about that next step you want to take. What does success look like? What next move gives you more of what your want—your next Champagne popping milestone?

  _____

  _____

- Step 2. Create a plan to get you from current place to your next Champagne popping milestone:
  o Define who to talk to.

  _____

  _____

  _____

o Synthesize your message to them.
   What's your proposal?

   _____

   _____

   Why are you interested in it?

   _____

   _____

   More importantly, why should they be interested?

   _____

   _____

o Determine how to approach them.
   When will I start the conversation(s)? _____
   Where should it happen? _____
   How will the meeting(s) be structured? _____

   _____

- Start executing against your plan!
- Capture key lessons:
   o What worked well?

   _____

   _____

   o What didn't work as well? What can I do better next time?

   _____

   _____

CHAPTER 13

Learn From All Leaders

Nothing goes to waste on the journey of life. Both good and bad experiences shape your mind and heart for what is to come.
—Leon Brown, retired Major League Baseball player

Why Should You?

Now you are steering the wheel of your own car on your way to Champagne! It's an amazing feeling. But you are not done. Drivers on a track are constantly getting input from what's happening around them; Their instrument panel, steering wheel vibration, engine noises, and crew commentary through their earpiece. With that input they can adjust, course correct, plan the next move, and so on. Similarly, your goal is to continuously become a better leader while on the road to Champagne. You will learn from things you did well, from things you did not do well, but also from seeing what other drivers do.

I've had many different bosses. Male or female, older or younger, down the hall or in a different continent, feared or truly admired, unknown or well-known in their industry, you name it. I have dealt with leaders (my direct boss or other) who displayed a wide range of behaviors I describe as inspiring, demotivating, innovative, square, empowering, micromanaging, respectful, bullying, efficient, distracting, caring, or indifferent. Note, I am describing their behaviors, not necessarily their character. Behaviors can be contrary to one's character—and misaligned with a professional brand—when not managed well.

Emotional intelligence (EI) is composed of two parts:[1]

- Personal competence
- Social competence

---

[1] T. Bradberry, and J. Greaves. 2009. *Emotional Intelligence 2.0.* TalentSmart.

Personal competence, has two components, which we explored in Chapter 6:

1. **Self-awareness** (accurately perceiving how you are wired). It's about understanding your emotions, preferences, strengths, and other components of the Self-Awareness Puzzle.
2. **Self-management** (learning to control your behavior). It's about biting your tongue or behaving strategically in ways that help you in the long-term ... even if exploding gives you short-term satisfaction.

Personal competence is about you, but social competence is about how you deal with others. We touched on it in Chapters 6 and 11. Social competence also consists of two components:

1. **Social awareness** (accurately perceiving what others are feeling). It's about listening to others and putting yourself in their shoes.
2. **Relationship management** (managing interactions well). It's about building and maintaining positive and healthy relationships.

When you are proficient at all four parts of EI, you obviously have high EI and therefore you are in a better position to be an admired person and leader in your field. You know ... the type of people others want to follow and the type that is given more. EI also helps you create better relationships, a key ingredient in your career's success. "If connecting with people isn't the most important skill you can have—now more than ever—I don't know what is!" Maria Pinelli, former Global Vice Chair at EY, told me during a podcast conversation.

But how do you increase your EI? There are multiple ways, and I believe resources like Emotional Intelligence 2.0 and the likes are a good place to start your research. But one method I want to share with you is free and simple: Observation! Every day, observe leaders around you in action and determine what they are doing right and what they are not. How does it feel to be led by them? What should they do differently to be more effective?

John C. Maxwell states "Leadership is more caught than taught. How does one 'catch' leadership? By watching good leaders in action! The majority of leaders emerge because of the impact made on them by established leaders who modeled leadership and mentored them."[2] That's exactly right.

However, I would go further and state that not only admirable leaders can teach you valuable lessons. Learn from all of them, even the ones you hate and can't stand, for they are constantly teaching you how *not* to treat others—they are perfect anti-role models; "*These are uninspirational people who show you the path to avoid. There are those who teach the perils of perfectionism, or not to be vile to colleagues.*"[3] As your career takes you to new levels of responsibility, which is a real consequence of wanting more in your career and applying the previous 12 Principles, continue developing and sharpening your own leadership style. To excel and grow in your field you must effectively lead others.

Learning from all leaders perhaps seems obvious, but not everyone is constantly doing it. I believe there are several reasons why, including:

- We believe we already know what it takes to be an admired leader.
- We filter out those leaders who we don't admire—especially the jerks—and dismiss the possibility of learning anything useful from them.
- It takes attention and energy to be in constant learning mode.

All leaders I worked with taught me lessons. Some lessons were extremely nice to learn and all I had to do was try to imitate their effective and empathetic ways. Some lessons were shocking, and I learned *not* to imitate them. Right now, you have role models and anti-role models in your personal and professional lives. No need to sign-up for training, just pay attention to their free lessons in a meeting near you.

Hinesh Shah, Vice President of Sales at Diageo, made an insightful addition to this concept during our podcast recording: "Whatever style you wish to adopt, whatever leader you want to be, whatever leader you

---

[2] J.C. Maxwell. 2007. *The 21 Irrefutable Laws of Leadership.* Thomas Nelson.
[3] E. Jacobs. March 01, 2020. "Stuff the inspiring types, find me an anti-role model." *Financial Times.* www.ft.com/content/2039ae88-58c6-11ea-abe5-8e03987b7b20 (accessed August 2020).

admire … it needs to come back and it needs to be authentic to you and who you are, which is grounded in your own personal values and norms." Don't just imitate. Incorporate those best practice leadership styles you admire into your style in a way that is authentic to who you are, so they are sustainable and natural to showcase.

Let me share a few of my career lessons because you can all learn from them too, as you strive to become an admired leader in your organization and field. Like Otto von Bismarck said, "Only a fool learns from his own mistakes. The wise man learns from the mistakes of others." Below is a sampling of unforgettable lessons I've learned from leaders around me that helped shape my leadership style.

Help Others

When new to an organization, I expand my network by scheduling meet-and-greet sessions with several executives. I want to introduce myself, learn about them, and welcome their advice as I settle into the new role: Seems like a good agenda to get the conversation going, perhaps initiate a new relationship, right?

So, I met this guy who started working at that company over 20 years ago, and he talked about his experience. Then I explained my background, and I asked him if he had any advice for a new colleague trying to succeed in the organization. He coldly replied, "I only help those who help me," gave me no advice, and the conversation awkwardly wrapped up soon after. What!? I did not expect that. I walked away puzzled because I hadn't heard a more selfish statement in a professional setting … at least not as impactful or memorable as that one.

Lesson: Giving others a word of advice does not cost you anything. Do not help others out of pure self-interest, do it because it is satisfying to help. If you want to be extremely selfish, think of this: You never know who you will need help from in the future—keep your options open.

Do Care

I told Stephen I would leave the office for a few hours that week. I explained I would become a U.S. citizen, and would attend my naturalization ceremony with my wife. He showed up at my ceremony! He went there because he realized it was a significant personal milestone and wanted to share the happy moment. I found out he did the same for another colleague many years ago and showed up at other public celebratory events like graduations. Show your team and peers that you sincerely care for them and you are there for them in good times and in bad times.

Earlier in my career, I told another manager that my wrists were starting to hurt due to carpal tunnel syndrome symptoms. I asked him for a better desk since my cheap one didn't allow the right ergonomic posture and angle. Instead of showing empathy and approving it, he told me a quick surgery fixed his sister's issue and therefore I should look into it.

Lesson: Demonstrate empathy toward your team, it goes a long way.

Be Respectful

We were in a small group of about five colleagues. We were reviewing technical specs of equipment and the most senior guy suddenly started screaming at me, in front of the rest. I can't even remember what he yelled about, just that my blood started to boil. He had an established reputation for being extremely tough and he was feared. As a bully hater, I yelled right back at him (debatable move, I admit); "You don't have to yell at me because I can hear you well! And you are not going to treat me like that!" I didn't know if I would see a punch coming at me or what. He calmed down and we kept discussing the topic like normal people. He never disrespected me again. That episode was unnecessary, he could have gotten his point across in a respectful manner, even if the message is firm and urgent.

Lesson: Treat others the way you want to be treated. And as a corollary, set the bar for how you will be treated. I've never yelled at a colleague or teammate, probably because I learned how it feels on the receiving end.

Be Accountable

I went into the client's office restroom after a key meeting and heard something I never heard before: A grown man crying in an office bathroom stall. I recognized Sam's (not his real name) shoes and immediately turned around and walked out. Sam was the junior partner I worked for in that project. Twenty minutes later, he came into the team room and

I didn't mention the restroom incident, because I did not want him to know that I knew and embarrass him even more.

Before running into him in the bathroom, we were in the same important meeting: Sam presented to multiple key executives, but the meeting went downhill—way downhill. They were not buying what he explained, and the client CEO grew extremely frustrated and annoyed. Our senior consulting partner stood up, walked to the front, and confidently stated: "Please ignore what Sam has been saying, it makes no sense, I know. What I propose we do is ..." Wow, he threw Sam under the bus in front of the consulting team and the client team and tried to be the hero. He could have rescued the conversation without destroying Sam's reputation. At the end of the day, as the senior partner, he was accountable for the team's performance and presentation.

Lesson: A leader takes a bullet for the team. Not only did he crush his teammate, he lost my respect and probably others'.

Clarify Expectations

I asked the project manager I joined that week, what role he wanted me to play in next week's workshop (i.e., lead or support, plus specifics). He started at the client two weeks before the rest of the team joined him, had already collected information, and planned this cross-functional diagnostic workshop to explore what did not work well between sales and supply chain that led to many inefficiency symptoms. He responded, "I'll lead it, and you can support me with this and that." Got it.

That's what we did, and the workshop went well. A few days later, a partner who attended the workshop (and who had interviewed me) told me; "I am deeply disappointed you did not lead the workshop, I thought you were going to show drive and initiative." Whoa, I never was aware about such expectations, given the project manager's clear direction. He made me feel awful for the long 45 minutes that tough session lasted, but more importantly, for many months because I felt I had a reputation to repair.

Lesson: As a manager or leader, you should clearly communicate your expectations because people are not mind readers. Since then, I make a concrete effort to ensure my team has clarity about my expectation of them in each mission: Only then can I gauge their performance.

Empower Your Team

The entry into the Brazilian chocolate market still is one of my most memorable and fulfilling projects. One of the many reasons is because my boss Carlos empowered me from the start. Carlos lived in Buenos Aires and I lived in São Paulo. He literally couldn't stop by my office every two hours to check how things were going; I saw him perhaps every three weeks. He gave me the space I needed to run my show as I saw fit, and to make many decisions. I involved him when I needed guidance or clarity, and to keep him informed as needed. This dynamic felt perfect for me, for it allowed me to further develop as a leader overseeing six workstreams and over 25 people on a day-to-day basis.

A friend with a similar profile as mine told me his boss wants to proof-read e-mails before they are sent out to executives to ensure there is nothing inappropriate in the tone, grammar, or content ... yikes.

Lesson: Build your team with qualified trustworthy people, clarify expectations, and get out the way. Let them grow.

Be Balanced

Growing up in Honduras, I would not see my father several days a week since he traveled to different parts of the country to build bridges. He built almost 100 bridges and was a key figure in developing the infrastructure of the country. When he was home, he would stop whatever he was doing to enjoy dinner with the family at the dinner table. *Absolutely nothing* would get in the way of dinner ... it was sacred family time. We would all sit at the table and enjoy a nice time together (even if conversations went south sometimes, like in all families). After the dinner table was cleared, he would spread out his blueprints, payroll documents, calculator, and so on, to work until he finished what he needed to finish that day. I would come by hours later to kiss him good night before going to bed, because I had school the next morning.

This taught me a couple of things: (1) work hard to accomplish my daily goals, and (2) there is more to life than work and I need to mind those aspects as well (time with my family, exercising, resting, learning, and so on). This first lesson is related to the value of hard work he instilled in me which I mentioned in Chapter 7. To this day, I prefer to pause work activities to exercise and have dinner, then I continue working—instead of working nonstop and sacrificing exercise and family dinner.

Lesson: Work diligently to finish what needs to be finished, don't fall behind. But there's so much more to life than your work deliverables!

Celebrate Success

After many months of working on a project that resulted in huge benefits for our company, Stephen told me "Great work on that project, AC, please take your wife to an upscale restaurant, have some of our nice Champagne and wine with dinner, and expense it." He does that for milestones for each teammate. It's a little detail, but it not only rewards the employee who performed well, it also increases the appreciation of the significant other who feels included as part of the team's effort and celebrations.

Lesson: Celebrating success is important, even milestones along the way toward the goal line. Of course, that is the whole point of *The Road to Champagne*: how to unlock growth achievements in your career that are worth celebrating (not just an end destination)! Construct a life full of events that trigger celebrations.

> *First things first. Get the Champagne.*
> —Winston Churchill, British prime minister (1874–1965)

I am sure you also have your own impactful stories: We all do.

So, what have all of these and other lessons done to my leadership style? Well, they influenced it, of course. My leadership style is one that:

- Clarifies the mission upfront and allows space for creativity and even mistakes
- Connects with the team as important individuals
- Empowers the team
- Is accessible and willing to help at any moment
- Is flexible depending on the needs of each team member
- Rolls up sleeves to work side-by-side with the team
- Helps each team member grow professionally toward their goals
- Holds others accountable, just as I am accountable

- Celebrates success
- Promotes fun

These characteristics didn't happen randomly. I chose what I believe are characteristics of someone I would love to follow by experiencing them as a follower. I am not imitating one person, the sum of all of them defines Alejandro's authentic leadership style; They all were picked up from different sources and experiences along the way. Your leadership style should consider what your followers want to experience.

Leadership is not about me. It is all about them.
—Dr. Marshall Goldsmith, top-rated executive coach and
bestselling author

Wrap-Up

Although this is the last chapter, this principle applies *now* wherever you are in your journey. All the leaders around me were highly intelligent, indeed. The key variable that made them awesome or not is their EI. One or few episodes of weak EI is enough to land you in somebody's blacklist and damage your professional brand. You will have poor and awesome leaders throughout your career. Don't waste the ugly lessons, they are teaching you how not to be; thus, apply the opposite to your life. And replicate the great lessons. That knowledge will make you a better leader—and driver on your road to success—every day.

Every experience, good or bad, is a priceless collector's item.
—Isaac Marion, American writer

Take-Aways: Learn From All Leaders

- EI is critical. Invest time and effort to increase it.
- Both role models and anti-role models teach you valuable lessons.
- Don't let a bad experience with your manager go to waste, learn how you can avoid it when leading others.

Self-Assessment

Which statement describes you best? Circle the corresponding letter.

a. I am not carefully paying attention to the leaders around me. Each of us has our own style. I have nothing to learn from poor leaders.

b. I learn from the good leaders around me, of course. But I mentally block the poor leaders, so they don't influence me.

c. I constantly assess leaders around me and take note of what to imitate and what to do the opposite of. This helps refine my leadership style. My EI is work-in-progress.

Actions

- Write down a list of the *best* leadership behavior examples you've witnessed.

_____

_____

_____

_____

_____

_____

- Circle those you want to make a visible part of your professional brand and leadership style.
- For each circled example, list concrete actions you will take to practice such behavior and embed it in your way of working.

Behavior: Action: Target date:

_____   _____   _____

_____   _____   _____

_____   _____   _____

_____   _____   _____

_____   _____   _____

_____   _____   _____

- Write down a list of the *worst* leadership behavior examples you've witnessed:

_____

_____

_____

_____

_____

- Circle those you never want to have associated with your professional brand.
- For each circled example, list concrete actions you will take to practice the opposite of such behavior and embed in your way or working (think about what to do to learn, practice, and embed such behavior in your way of working). If opposite behavior is addressed in the previous page, no need include below.

Behavior: Action: Target date:

_____   _____   _____

_____   _____   _____

_____   _____   _____

_____   _____   _____

_____   _____   _____

_____   _____   _____

Self-Assessment

The goal of this book is not only to expose you to actions that will attack root causes of slow career growth, but also to help you prioritize where to focus your efforts. You will do that with a few simple steps:

a. Go back to the Self-Assessment at the end of each chapter. If you skipped it, that's not going to work … go back and do it.
b. Find the statement you circled (the one that you relate to more).
c. Write the letter of each circled statement:
   o Principle 1: _____
   o Principle 2: _____
   o Principle 3: _____
   o Principle 4: _____
   o Principle 5: _____
   o Principle 6: _____
   o Principle 7: _____
   o Principle 8: _____
   o Principle 9: _____
   o Principle 10: _____
   o Principle 11: _____
   o Principle 12: _____
   o Principle 13: _____
d. Color or mark inside each segment of the framework in Figure 0.1, with markers or pens, using this key:
   o A = red
   o B = yellow
   o C = green
e. This is the key for each letter:
   o A = Beginner (you have not embedded this principle)
   o B = Intermediate (you have good proficiency but must improve further)
   o C = Master (you are very proficient at living this principle!)

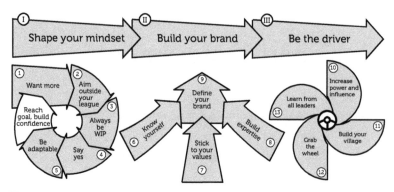

Figure 0.1 The Road to Champagne© Framework

   f. Now you can visually appreciate which principles you need to focus
     your improvement efforts on:

     o Start by working toward eliminating any red areas.

     o Then focus on converting the yellow areas to green.

     o Finally, don't neglect the green areas. The definition of "Master"
       evolves as you grow, requiring you to continue sharpening that
       principle.

   g. Start executing against your improvement plan for the prioritized
     areas.

In case you are curious, the self-assessments polls from participants in
speeches I've given in multiple countries (from high school juniors all
the way to my peers) reveal a few themes:

- The top three principles they say they need to focus
  on are:
  - Principle 9, Define Your Brand
  - Principle 12, Grab the Wheel
  - Principle 2, Aim Outside Your League

If you currently have a good level of proficiency in any principle, know
that the bar likely rises in your next position, requiring you to elevate your
proficiency level. This means you must be WIP in all! Becoming green
in all 13 principles is possible but will take time, effort, and conscious

attention. That's why I said in the introduction that the younger you start addressing these areas, the smoother your journey will be—but it's never too late (unless you are retiring next month).

The less red or yellow you have, the higher your likelihood of success ... so get to work so you can pop Champagne bottles sooner rather than later!

Conclusion

Congratulations! You deserve popping open a bottle of Champagne because you made it to the end of the book! Hopefully reading this book triggers a new vision of a better version of You flourishing in your career … and you are strategizing about concrete steps to make it happen.

Together we have explored 13 basic yet powerful ways to maximize the effectiveness of your journey toward success. Remember this is not a sprint, it's an endurance race that should last for as long as your career does. Because many of these principles require *a lot of effort,* it is fair to assume not many will have the discipline and drive to effectively apply them all—don't let that be you, give it your best shot! It will also not be a linear pass through the 13 actionable principles and you may need to focus on some principles more than on others at different times.

The objective is to use them all to continue elevating yourself toward an improved version of You in your career and life. Using these principles is embarking on a continuously evolving and thrilling journey, but you must start now.

To Shape Your Mindset, You Must ...

1. Want more out of your career and life, or else they can stagnate. Desire brings momentum to overcome inertia. But enjoy each phase.
2. Aim outside your league, don't aspire to the normal and expected. Go big!
3. Shift your mindset and attitude to one of continuous learning and always be WIP, never a finished product. Otherwise, you become stale and miss out on potential exciting opportunities.
4. Say yes to stretch assignments, challenges, or opportunities more often. It will more than likely bring positive outcomes on a personal and/or professional level.
5. Be adaptable to succeed in different environments, wherever those opportunities take you. Expect change because that comes with "more." Better yet, proactively seek it.

To Build Your Brand, You Must ...

6. Know yourself inside-out with sharp accuracy: What defines you and how others perceive you. Only then can you learn to manage yourself and shape yourself into the leader you want to become.
7. Stick to your values and let them guide your decision making. First you must be in tune with your value set.
8. Build expertise in one or two key topics that will differentiate you in your field. Be known for mastering such topic(s). Ensure you have adequate performance on other relevant topics in your field: Avoid glaring weaknesses.
9. Bring the three elements above into a cohesive and brief brand statement conveying your value-proposition. Invest in building and maintaining that brand, and letting it evolve in a conscious and strategic manner to the next-level You.

To Be the Driver, You Must ...

10. Know the power dynamics of the world you operate in to be more effective in your role. Learn to be influential to move the right solutions forward.

11. Build your village because it does take one to see you through each goal line. Your career is not an individual sport, so build the right relationships and network. Use the influence and relationships you build to help others grow as well.

12. Grab the steering wheel of your career. Forget passively relying on others to make it happen for you. They won't do it, or they can take you down a path inconsistent with your values, aspirations, or brand. This is one responsibility you must not delegate.

13. Learn from all leaders around you: The good, the bad, the ugly. They all are teaching you how to be and how not to be. If one negatively impacts you, understand how to be the opposite with your followers and peers. Invest in your emotional intelligence.

As I mentioned, these principles have taken me on an exciting journey across the food and beverage industry in multiple countries and allowed me to reach an exciting phase working with Champagne brands I love. Having worked with chocolate, candy, gum, low-calorie toppings, banana pureé, shrimp, cookies, and hamburgers, I can certainly say I prefer the current product samples. Working with strategy, problem-solving, fine Champagnes, and living in a tropical city of my choosing makes me firmly believe these principles work. Putting these principles into action has helped my life and the lives of many friends, colleagues, and even family members mentioned in this book, including Alex, Alison, Eric, Guillermo, Hector, Hinesh, Jasmin, Juan, Lili, Lindsey, Maria, Mariela, Neeraj, Phil, Rissa, and so many other guests of The Road to Champagne podcast, plus so many others I could not mention.

Test the 13 Principles. Success is never guaranteed, but these are ways to maximize the probability you arrive at your Champagne. This is what this book is about. Whether this was a refresher or new information, my hope is to motivate you to make the necessary adjustments to your mindset, your brand positioning, and your actions to transform you into an improved and more successful version of you. Propel your career forward. Now you are better armed to ponder "How can I continue growing in my career? How can I make the next interesting move happen?" which I propose you ask every few years in case you need to take corrective action to get to more. Otherwise, you won't improve your present stage, especially if there is more potential inside of you to create more value and impact. Eventually, your current place may no longer be the best place.

Each chapter contained a set of Actions. Go back in case you skipped them—or download the fillable templates from www.RoadToChampagne. com. And listen to the podcasts where you can hear my interviewees—the ones you read about—tell you their stories and perspectives directly, at www.RoadToChampagne.com/podcasts/ (or wherever you listen to podcasts).

I wish you the best, and I thank you for your support. Cheers to your success!

Success is no accident. It is hard work, perseverance, learning, studying, sacrifice and most of all, love of what you are doing or learning to do.

—Pelé

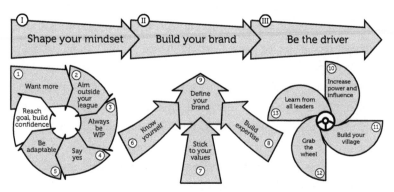

Figure C.1 The Road to Champagne© framework

References

Afremow, J. 2013. *The Champion's Mind*. Rodale.

Algoe, S.B., et al. 2010. "It's the Little Things: Everyday Gratitude as a Booster Shot For Romantic Relationships." *Personal Relationships* 17, pp. 217–233.

Bartleby. October 10, 2019. "In Praise of Dissenters." *The Economist*. www.economist.com/business/2019/10/10/in-praise-of-dissenters (accessed June 2020).

Bradberry, T., and J. Greaves. 2009. *Emotional Intelligence 2.0*. TalentSmart.

Casciaro, T., and M.S. Lobo. June 2005. "Competent Jerks, Lovable Fools, and the Formation of Social Networks." *Harvard Business Review*.

Christensen, L., et al. August 2020. "The most fundamental skill: Intentional learning and the career advantage." *McKinsey Accelerate*. www.mckinsey.com/featured-insights/future-of-work/the-most-fundamental-skill-intentional-learning-and-the-career-advantage (accessed September 2020).

Cross, R., and R. Thomas. July–August 2011. "A Smarter Way To Network." *Harvard Business Review*.

Davis, I., D. Keeling, P. Schreier, and A. Williams. July 2007. "The McKinsey Approach to Problem Solving." *McKinsey Staff Paper*, No. 66.

Diaz-Uda, A., C. Medina, and B. Schill. July 24, 2013. "Diversity's New Frontier." *Deloitte Insights*.

Disalvo, D. August 20, 2018. "Can Personality Change or Does It Stay The Same For Life? A New Study Suggests It's A Little of Both." *Forbes.com*. www.forbes.com/sites/daviddisalvo/2018/08/20/can-personality-change-or-does-it-stay-the-same-for-life-a-new-study-says-its-a-little-of-both/?sh=5d96c1f79caa (accessed August 2020).

Dweck, C.S. 2016. *Mindset: The New Psychology of Success*. Ballantine Books.

Emmons, R.A., and M.E. McCullough. 2003. "Counting Blessings Versus Burdens: An Experimental Investigation of Gratitude and Subjective Well-Being in Daily Life." *The Journal of Personality and Social Psychology* 84, no.2, pp. 377–389.

Ericsson, K.A., M.J. Prietula, and E.T. Cokely. July–August 2007. "The Making of an Expert" *Harvard Business Review*.

Eurich, T. January 04, 2018. "What Self-Awareness Really Is (and How to Cultivate It)." *Harvard Business Review*.

Eurich, T. October 19, 2018. "Working with People Who Aren't Self-Aware." *Harvard Business Review*.

Gebelein, S.H., et al. 2001. *Successful Manager's Handbook*. Personnel Decisions International.

Greene, R. 2000. *The 48 Laws of Power*. Penguin Books.

Hewlett, S.A. 2013. *(Forget a Mentor) Find a Sponsor*. Harvard Business Review Press.

Houston, B. 2018. *There Is More.* WaterBrook.

Hunt, V., S. Prince, S. Dixon-Fyle, and K. Dolan. May 19, 2020. "Diversity wins: How inclusion matters." *McKinsey & Co.* www.mckinsey.com/featured-insights/diversity-and-inclusion/diversity-wins-how-inclusion-matters (accessed August 2020).

Innes, R.H. 1998. "Hernan Cortes." *Brittanica.* www.britannica.com/biography/Hernan-Cortes (accessed July 2020)

Jacobs, E. March 01, 2020. "Stuff the inspiring types, find me an anti-role model." *Financial Times.* www.ft.com/content/2039ae88-58c6-11ea-abe5-8e03987b7b20 (accessed August 2020).

Jeffrey Pfeffer. 1992. *Managing with Power.* Harvard Business School Press.

John E. Sheridan, et al. 2017. "Effects of Corporate Sponsorship and Departmental Power on Career Tournaments." *Academy of Management.*

Johnson, S. 2000. *Who Moved My Cheese?* Penguin Random House.

MacNeil, K. 2015. *The Wine Bible.* Workman Publishing.

Maxwell, J.C. 2007. *The 21 Irrefutable Laws of Leadership.* Thomas Nelson.

Michaelson, G. 2003. *Sun Tzu For Success.* Adams Media.

Mills, P.J., et al. 2015. "The Role of Gratitude in Spiritual Well-being in Asymptomatic Heart Failure Patients." *Spirituality in Clinical Practice* 2, No. 1, pp. 5–17. American Psychological Association.

Murphy, M. August 14, 2016. "The Big Reason Why Some People Are Terrified of Change (While Others Love It)." *Forbes.com.* www.forbes.com/sites/markmurphy/2016/08/14/the-big-reason-why-some-people-are-terrified-of-change-while-others-love-it/?sh=120d85392f63 (accessed June 2020).

Nemeth, C.J. 2018. *In Defense of Troublemakers–The Power of Dissent in Life and Business.* Hachette Book Group.

Phillips, K.W. September 18, 2017. "How Diversity Makes Us Smarter." *Greater Good Magazine.* https://greatergood.berkeley.edu/article/item/how_diversity_makes_us_smarter (accessed May 2020).

Power, Influence, and Persuasion. 2005. Harvard Business School Press.

Reproduced with permission from MindTools.com. 2020. *What Are Your Values?* [Online]. Available from: www.mindtools.com/community/pages/article/newTED_85.htm. (accessed June 2020).

Steward, D.L. 2004. *Doing Business By The Good Book.* Hyperion.

Wood, A.M., et al. January 2009. "Gratitude Influences Sleep Through the Mechanism of Pre-sleep Cognitions." *Journal of Psychosomatic Research* 66, No. 1, pp. 43–48.

www.Gracefund.org

www.hectorastorga.com

Zitelmann, R. December 30, 2019. "Set More Ambitious Goals This New Year's Eve!" *Forbes.com.* www.forbes.com/sites/rainerzitelmann/2020/12/30/set-more-ambitious-goals-this-new-years-eve/?sh=7798bcd73d00 (accessed June 2020).

Website

Please visit www.RoadToChampagne.com

There you can:

Download the free Actions templates in fillable pdf format

Listen to podcasts with guest speakers exploring each principle!

Join our mailing list to download a pdf of the framework …
perfect to print and place where you can see it every day.

Send Alejandro your comments

Social Media

Please follow us on social media:

- LinkedIn: Search for *The Road to Champagne*
- Instagram: Search for *The Road to Champagne*
- Facebook: Search for *The Road to Champagne*
- YouTube: Search for *The Road to Champagne* channel

About the Author

Alejandro Colindres Frañó is a food and beverage executive with extensive experience in the industry after working in leading companies including McKinsey & Company, Kearney, Cadbury (now Mondelēz), Restaurant Brands International and others in the United States, Brazil, and Honduras. Currently, he is Vice President of Strategy and Commercial Effectiveness at Southern Glazer's Wine & Spirits, a privately held company with sales over $20B. Alejandro obtained his bachelor's degree from Cornell University and his MBA from Kellogg School of Management at Northwestern University.

He brings together 30+ years of life lessons under a simple framework to allow the reader to think strategically about maximizing success in their own career and life. His passions include traveling around the world, running, the beach, and wines. He lives in Miami with his wife and their doggy.

Index

Concise and Applied Business Books

The Collection listed above is one of 30 business subject collections that Business Expert Press has grown to make BEP a premiere publisher of print and digital books. Our concise and applied books are for...

- Professionals and Practitioners
- Faculty who adopt our books for courses
- Librarians who know that BEP's Digital Libraries are a unique way to offer students ebooks to download, not restricted with any digital rights management
- Executive Training Course Leaders
- Business Seminar Organizers

Business Expert Press books are for anyone who needs to dig deeper on business ideas, goals, and solutions to everyday problems. Whether one print book, one ebook, or buying a digital library of 110 ebooks, we remain the affordable and smart way to be business smart. For more information, please visit www.businessexpertpress.com, or contact sales@businessexpertpress.com.